NOBODY'S VICTIM

Other Books by
Christopher McCullough, Ph.D.
Always at Ease
Managing Your Anxiety

NOBODY'S VICTIM

Freedom from Therapy and Recovery

CHRISTOPHER J. MCCULLOUGH, PH.D.
WITH KRISTIN ANUNDSEN

Clarkson Potter/Publishers
New York

Published by Clarkson N. Potter/Publishers, 201 East 50th Street, New York, New York 10022. Member of the Crown Publishing Group.
Random House, Inc. New York, Toronto, London, Sydney, Auckland
CLARKSON N. POTTER, POTTER, and colophon are trademarks of Clarkson N. Potter, Inc.
Manufactured in the United States
Design by Renato Stanisic
Library of Congress Cataloging-in-Publication Data

McCullough, Christopher J.
    Nobody's victim : freedom from therapy and recovery / by
Christopher J. McCullough with Kristin Anundsen. — 1st ed.
        p.   cm.
        1. Adjustment (Psychology)   2. Victims—Psychology.   3. Blame.
    4. Faultfinding.   5. Scapegoat—Psychological aspects.
    I. Anundsen, Kristin.   II. Title.
    BF335.4.M33   1995
    158'.1—dc20
                                                                94-45556
                                                                CIP

ISBN 0-517-59801-9
10 9 8 7 6 5 4 3 2 1
First Edition

My fine mother, Lydia Emma McCullough, and the memory of my father, Harold H. McCullough.

My mentor, Peter Koestenbaum, who I think knows everything.

Michael P. O'Connor, friend and artist extraordinaire.

My cousin, Bob Long, with whom I shared a joyous childhood.

and

The memory of Rollo May, whose heroic life in the pursuit of beauty and truth has inspired my life.

Contents

Acknowledgments

I always read, with keen interest, the Acknowledgments section of a book. It's a bit more personal than the text and often tells me whether the author had a dog to keep him or her company during late-night or early-morning writing sessions. And do any spouse and kids get credit for "putting up with" the writer's unpredictable and lengthy hours? Does the author give thanks to the editor or publisher, or have they had a falling-out by now? Does the author demonstrate a rigorous approach that drew in many others who reviewed and "made technical suggestions along the way"? Are there any "Most of all I'd like to thank Betty, my typist" comments? Any special people who "made it all possible"?

No matter how tedious the experience of writing the book was, the attitude in the Acknowledgments section is nearly always conciliatory, if not forgiving. I'm nobody's victim, mind you; this book you're about to read was a terrific experience. I found surprising connections among old ideas, tuned up my assumptions, and stretched for new awareness. You can't have more fun than that.

I don't have spouses, dogs, or children, not right now, but I have had the emotional and intellectual support of a very good few. In jumbled order:

My editor, Kristin Anundsen, whose mind works the opposite of mine: she's structured, organized, and coherent. My guardian angel, Patricia Evans, who gets extra credit for reading the manuscript all along the way and consistently saying it was wonderful; I hope she's right. Pamela Krauss, executive editor at Clarkson Potter, who green-lighted me to write this book and agreed that it would be good to go deeper than mere criticism. The people who risked asking me, "How is the book going?" My friends and colleagues at the Psychological Resource Center in Cary, North Carolina, for their support and love. My very fine agent, Dr. Sid Harriet, who sent me a Christmas card halfway through the writing that said, "I believe in you." Thanks, Sid.

And special thanks, as they say, to some great friends who have cared for me during terrific as well as troubled times: You know who you are.

Preface

In writing this book I discovered something unexpected in the way of a personal reprieve. I have always felt a slight twinge of embarrassment about what I jokingly refer to as my checkered educational past. I have obtained degrees or done serious study in psychology, sociology, pharmacology, philosophy, and psychotherapy. When I switched from psychology to sociology, because the scientific study of humans seemed absurd to me, I found that sociology also tried to objectify and predict the unpredictable. Missing in both disciplines was the appreciation for the deeper existential issues of life. Academic philosophy, too, seemed sterile in its disconnection from its early roots, when it pondered the question "What is the good life?"

This ongoing search, which felt at various times like adolescent confusion, and at other times like a semi-noble pursuit of truth, found resolution when I met professor and mentor Dr. Koestenbaum. As a well-respected—even adored—philosopher, he was, at the time I met him, applying philosophy to psychological issues, eventually referring to this pursuit as clinical philosophy. While applied or clinical philosophy is not defined by specific methods and techniques, it is characterized by its deepest claim that freedom is the essence of human potential. It asserts that much of what is passed off as psychological disorders, as well as lesser emotional suffering, are actually manifestations of our crippled awareness of freedom.

Even though I have used therapy and recovery to illustrate the issues of victimization, the ideas here are for everyone living the great dilemmas of our time. In writing *Nobody's Victim* I came to see how my own struggle for a satisfying academic synthesis mirrored, although more formally than most, a general yearning for what is missing, socially and spiritually, in our culture. We do not merely feel victimized by abusive parents, neurotic genes, or our own weakness of character; we suffer from a lack of community and from unsatisfying answers to life's great questions.

I believe that the growth of victimhood in America represents a symptom of important unmet needs in our society. Rather than confronting these needs, we try to patch the symptoms and have designed a huge industry that sells us on the promise of eliminating our emotional pain and emptiness. When we contemplate the harshness of the world—the greed of corporate takeover artists and savings-and-loan pillagers, the mindless violence that seems to erupt anywhere, the abuse that family members inflict on one another—it is easy to get discouraged. When that happens, we are likely to lose sight of what really has meaning for us. We then try to fill the void with such palliatives as consumerism, overwork, or therapy. Our own pleasure, problems, acquisitions, and image become substitutes for beauty, creativity, connectedness, and love.

Norman Lear, quoted in the *Washington Post*, put it this way: "Let's face it, we are not a nation enjoying its material success. And it should be obvious by now that a higher GNP, a faster computer chip, and interactive television with five hundred channels are not going to address the hole in America's heart, a direct result of the spiritual poverty of our time."

All of these factors have had a profound effect on my clinical practice and how I relate to those who find their way to my office. My practice of clinical philosophy is a marriage of existential philosophy, which is interested in the awareness and manifestation of free choice, and what some call the "spiritual" reality of emptiness from which all choice comes, and which forms the heart of Eastern thought.

As a practitioner and as a person, I feel that every human being is a generous, worldly manifestation of the mysterious void. Regardless of the specific suffering presented to me by a patient, I feel that my responsibility is not to analyze with an endless string of insights, but to be fully present and to remind the patient of the truth of his or her freedom. "Therapy," to the extent that it is the practice of insight and behavioral techniques, is not what I do. Whatever else I may do that may be called therapeutic, it comes from the fundamental fact that I can only remind people of what they already know. While the term *therapist* sounds more potent than *reminder,* the latter better reflects what I now do.

It is in this role of reminder that I came to write this book. It's my hope that it will shed light on the truth behind the victim syndrome and offer some general, as well as specific, ways to help you break free of old behavior and learn to embrace the more significant freedoms you'll be encountering in their place.

HOW WE COME TO FEEL LIKE VICTIMS

1

The Allure of Victimhood

Nancy had made, but canceled, several appointments to see me over the past three months. Finally she actually came in. Dressed just this side of down and out, she brushed back her long, unkempt, graying hair and sighed.

"I've tried to see if I could actually make it without therapy," she confessed. "On a good day I feel strong and cancel my appointment, but the next day I feel desperate to talk to someone. I guess you could say I'm one of those 'therapy junkies'—I've been in and out of one kind of treatment or another for over twenty years. Every new kind of therapy has seemed like the right answer at first, but I still feel empty and depressed."

"What issues were you dealing with in your therapies?" I asked.

"Well, in my Freudian analysis I talked a lot about my critical father and distant mother. In behavioral therapy we didn't talk about that at all; my therapist just kept saying that the past didn't matter, that I should just take some action to improve my life—

but I wasn't sure *what* action. It was really confusing. And I wasn't sure either of these shrinks understood me—they appeared to have perfect lives and perfect families, so how could they really know what I was going through?

"That's why support groups were such a revelation. I'd resisted going, since I'd never felt comfortable telling strangers my problems. But when I heard the others describe their emotional pain, I finally felt that I was not alone. These people seemed to care about me, which I don't think the therapists did, and I made friends for the first time since elementary school. Over the years I guess I've been in at least six different recovery groups, from Codependents Anonymous to Adult Children of Alcoholics."

She paused, looking uncomfortable. I waited for the "but."

"But you know what?" she asked mournfully. "Even though I felt secure in these groups, I never did get to the point where I really felt capable of being on my own. With all the work I've done, I still feel like a failure because I'm so dependent. It's depressing to be here today seeing you—no offense. Here I am back to square one, still feeling like a helpless victim."

Nancy was not the first patient I'd treated who had shuttled back and forth between psychotherapy and recovery programs, never finding satisfaction or substantially relieving their pain. (I use the term *patient* not as an implication of pathology but, rather, to indicate some degree of suffering. *Client* sounds too cold and businesslike for my taste.) And from her comments I sensed (an assessment confirmed by later sessions) that she had something else in common with the others: The circumstances that propelled her into treatment in the first place were not severe enough to justify the intensity and length of her therapy. After all, how many successful, confident people also grew up with critical fathers and distant mothers?

I've never felt that my patients were faking their pain and suffering; indeed, their misery is all too real. But when I compare the time and money spent on recovery and psychotherapy with the issues many of these men and women are grappling with, I wonder if they are not spinning their wheels—or worse, deepening their frustration and distress.

At no other time in American history have so many of us sensed that life is unfair, abusive, and unreasonably cruel. With nearly 50 million citizens diagnosed with some sort of mental disorder, countless numbers in support groups and recovery programs, and some five hundred new self-help and self-improvement books published each year, we appear—to a growing number of critics—to be creating a cult of emotional victims. It's no secret that victimhood is a large and growing fraternity. Although no one knows *how* large, exactly, it's easy to see that many of us have fallen into the victim mode. It has become woven into the national fabric; hair shirts are in. Among the recent phenomena indicating that victimhood is on the upswing:

• Hundreds of new self-help and addiction-oriented books appear every year, commanding entire sections in bookstores. Just when it seems impossible for someone to write another such book, along come dozens more, pointing out heretofore unrecognized sources of dysfunction and providing endless checklists, exercises, tips, and techniques that promise to free readers from their suffering. But if they are so effective, why all the sequels?

- Peer-based recovery organizations are proliferating like mice in a cornfield; overeaters, overspenders, workaholics, sexaholics, offspring of abusive or alcoholic parents—all find affinity/support groups that encourage them to relive their hurtful past . . . over and over again. People flock to psychotherapy and a proliferation of offshoots from breath work to aromatherapy to metapsychology. In fact, therapy and recovery are so popular that it's difficult to find any adult who has never participated in such treatments. If anyone feels wronged, a program exists to validate (and, theoretically, heal) the wounds.

- Stories and shows on abuse and recovery fill the airwaves, as men and women proclaim on network television that they've either come to terms with or cannot resolve their troubled pasts.

- Politicians, actors, athletes, and other public figures rush to confess having fallen victim to abuses of all kinds. They wear their victimhood like badges of honor, inspiring the admiration of those who idolize them.

Both the media and the psychological professions present such a strong message that all emotional pain is unacceptable that every ordinary human suffering is thought to be a bona fide illness, disease, disorder, or abnormality. In such a social climate, it's no surprise when even relatively happy individuals wonder if they, too, aren't recovering from *something*—or worse, in denial.

LOOKING FOR BLAME

People who define themselves as "victims" of this or that frequently end up feeling helpless and hopeless. In effect, they're announcing that some outside person or force has determined the course of their lives.

Assigning blame requires some kind of fixing or retaliation. The type of fixing the victim chooses depends on the identified victimizer. Some victims have no real outlet for their accusations because they blame otherworldly causes—God, fate, the stars, the supernatural—that cannot be effectively attacked. Earthquakes and floods cannot be "blamed" in the personal sense of implying that these victimizers acted with intention or choice. You can rail at inanimate objects, such as the nail that pierced your tire, thus causing the flat that made you late for your appointment, but you have to admit that you're being irrational. How much more satisfying it would be if you could find a *person* who placed the nail under your tire. Then you could take some action: confrontation, retaliation, magnanimous granting of absolution.

This victimizer can be one's parents, one's mate, the other gender, one's genes, the educational system, society in general. It's comforting to say we can't be responsible for our actions: We were abused! Our families were dysfunctional! Our inner children were deprived! Some other factor—gender, race, age, political group—held all the cards! How could anyone expect us to make anything out of our lives given the odds against us! If our lives are disappointments, if a relationship fails, if our career founders, it's not because of anything *we* did—is it?

When victims can identify a whole, warm-blooded victimizer, they usually choose to punish him or her (or it, if the culprit is, say, a dog that bit). They may lash out in violence or make a verbal attack. They may mount a campaign or initiate a lawsuit.

Sometimes they are more covert. "The fault, dear Brutus, is

not in our stars, but in ourselves, that we are underlings," says crafty Cassius, who then proceeds to plant the idea that Julius Caesar is in fact to blame, and is thus deserving of death. Remaining in misery—guilt-tripping—is another way for a victim to punish an abuser. To say that one has suffered pain at the hands of someone else satisfies the inherent urge to identify cause. But cause, in itself, does not define victimhood; blame does. Blame and victimhood say, "You have taken something from me and I can't feel good about myself until you confess and repent."

But comforting as it may be to assign blame for our travails, it is in no way a solution, and in the end it is cold comfort indeed if we are unable to make meaningful connections, pursue work and other interests that are sustaining, find a sense of peace with our world and our place in it.

Certainly, victimhood seems to have gotten completely out of hand. In fact, there is a growing number of critics who attack those who have fallen into the trap of victimhood, calling them whiners and wimps. But how can you blame people for seeking relief when they are clearly in pain? And who am I—or they—to declare whose pain is valid and whose is not? When we start analyzing the degrees of triviality and validity, we inevitably get into the old apples-and-oranges comparison dilemma. Moreover, we become participants in that very blame game we so deplore. (And where in the hierarchy do we place people like Nancy, who feels like a victim but doesn't ask the world to pay reparations?) Suffering always feels real to the sufferer, even if the cause of that pain seems frivolous to an outside observer.

If you are caught in the victim trap, you may have experienced anger or ridicule from friends or family who don't understand why you can't simply "let go of the past." But simply telling you to "grow up and get on with it" will not work for emotional problems any more than nagging works for an irresponsible teenager. Criticism and name-calling are not particularly effective ways to get Johnny to empty the trash or clean up his room. If Johnny's own needs are ignored, he is not likely to reform.

Understanding unmet needs must not be confused with coddling; Johnny needs to empty the trash regardless of whether or not his parents possess insight into his reluctance to do so. However, the nagger/nagged relationship is a stressful and unpleasant one. If, for example, Johnny needs and receives a feeling that he is valued and appreciated for helping out with the trash, he is less likely to feel oppressed by it. Likewise, when we have our legitimate needs met in more direct ways, we are better able to forsake the indirect path of victimhood.

Victims are not necessarily sniffling, immature whiners. Your despair feels genuine because it is genuine. But consider the possibility that you are not fully aware of the needs behind your particular emotional pain. Behind a drinking or drug problem, marital discord, sexual confusion, depression, anxiety, or anger, there may lie an emptiness you don't know how else to fill.

Until you delve *beneath* the behavior, you are stuck with treating the symptom (victimhood) as if it, in itself, were the problem. Rather than asking, "Who is to blame for my unhappiness?," it might be more useful to take a step back and inquire, "Why do I feel like a victim, and what is it doing for me? What needs am I attempting to meet, and is there any other way to meet them besides psychotherapy, recovery, and acting out?"

What Victimhood Offers

Make no mistake: The pull of victimhood can be very strong. Apart from the political and financial advantages of forming factions and being able to sue for grievances, victimhood offers, or appears to offer, certain psychological rewards: Why wouldn't the claim of being abused and victimized be appealing to us in a world that does not attend to some of our most basic psychological needs? Moreover, I think that victimhood is a pretty intelligent choice even though an ultimately inadequate one. We need not feel guilty for trying the best way we know how to get our legitimate needs met. Let's look at some of the appealing characteristics of victimhood.

1. Victims receive care and attention. Being seen, heard, and loved are among the most basic human needs. We learn very early in life that if we fall off a swing and skin our knee or get pinched by Suzy, someone is likely to comfort us. Many children try to prolong this loving attention by milking their victimhood. Wise parents learn to pick up on that ploy and say something like, "You're okay now, go out and play." Adults seek caring in recovery groups and in the offices of professional healers, although such treatment programs rarely let them know they're now okay.

2. The victim's own destructive behavior is obscured. The child who successfully sells his or her pain to a parent is often the one who appears most hurt in the situation. Johnny may look more pitiful than Suzy, but Johnny may have tormented Suzy for some time before she pinched him. In recovery and psychotherapy the abusers are phantoms; therapists and support group peers know them only through the perceptions of the "victim." The patient's own perception of his or her role in the situation becomes distorted through repeated tellings of the victim tale. Thus, victimhood protects another basic human need: self-esteem.

3. Victims are justified in not exercising their responsibility. Freedom of choice is a birthright Americans have died defending. On the other hand, it is also a natural burden. We must repeatedly choose, and even though we can never know all the consequences of our choices, beforehand or even afterward, we still remain totally responsible for them. However, if we are not free—if others have us in their power—we are relieved of this heavy burden of responsibility. Of course, the price of this relief is loss of freedom; without responsibility we react to life rather than take charge of it. But to some sufferers this price does not seem too high. Freedom from responsibility appears to provide some relief from the risks and pressures of contemporary life, at least temporarily.

4. Victims may feel power over their abusers. Parading your suffering in front of your abuser is a forceful way of punishing that person. Even if the abuser fails to show remorse, you can use victimhood as an ongoing reminder, to yourself and your therapist or recovery group, that the abuser deserves opprobrium and punishment. Beneath this desire to punish lie desires for power, self-validation, self-acceptance, and acceptance by others.

Sonya came to see me because she had been unsuccessful in losing weight. She had tried nearly all the diet programs available, and then someone had suggested that there might be an emotional component to the poundage problem. It turned out that throughout Sonya's childhood, her mother had criticized her for being overweight, even when Sonya wasn't. I asked her to imagine herself at a weight she thought her mother would approve of, and to feel how happy both she and her mother would be. Sonya turned red and said with great anger, "I wouldn't give her the pleasure after the way she treated me." For Sonya to be slim and happy was, in her mind, to let her mother off the hook. Only her continuing misery gave her power over her mother's abuse.

5. Victimhood can help you avoid dealing with other fundamental issues of life. While in the safe haven of victimhood, you do not have to clean your room. A focus on the victimized state, and the stories that validate it, keeps you from dealing with other important concerns. While you work hard to get your victim support needs met, you may feel justified in neglecting family and business responsibilities, not to mention the deeper philosophical questions of meaning and spirituality. As long as your inner child is in distress, you do not have to grow up and face the troublesome complexities of adulthood.

6. Victims can share a feeling of belonging and connection. Not only does misery love company, we all love company. Unfortunately, we live in a society that seriously lacks caring, supportive community. As a result, a growing number of people are looking for fellowship in support groups and therapy groups, where there are plenty of people eager to commiserate, to claim similar backgrounds and confess to similar failings. Cults represent an extreme manifestation of the need to belong: Anything, even total submission to a cultic credo or identification by a common pathology, is better than isolation.

Once, community could be taken for granted. Families stuck together, right or wrong, and neighbors could be counted on to help one another out. However, in our relentless pursuit of individualism and mobility, we have lost that sense of community. People are distanced—physically and psychologically—from their families of origin, and divorces split up their chosen families. Today, one in four people live alone. Even intact families move so often that it's difficult to put down roots in a neighborhood. As a result, we feel disconnected and lonely.

If evolving past the victim role means being tossed back into isolation, small wonder so many are reluctant to try.

7. *Wearing the badge of victimhood creates a sense of identity where one is missing.* Those who think that "Who am I?" is just an idle question should be urged to try answering it. Our culture has become so outer-directed that we are defined by our function: what we do. One of my patients, echoing the plaints of actors and sports figures, told me, "I feel that I'm only as good as my last performance." We have, as a culture, become estranged from the certitude of the inner self.

FEEDING OUR HUNGER

Extreme other-directedness and people-pleasing creates, in our society, a terrible emptiness. It is not surprising that we turn inward to reclaim a lost sense of self—that authentic self that has been lost in the marketplace. We are so wrapped up in trying to market ourselves to employers, friends, romantic interests, and so on that we are unsure of who is really inside. The intense competition created by technological advances and narrowing job opportunities has not helped. Performance has, indeed, replaced authenticity as a measure of our humanity; keeping up hinders us from disclosing, even experiencing, our essence.

Psychologist Philip Cushman attributes this emptiness in part to broad historical forces such as industrialization, urbanization, and secularism. "Our terrain," he says, "has shaped a self that experiences a significant absence of community, tradition, and shared meaning. It experiences these social absences and their consequences 'interiorly' as a lack of personal conviction and worth, and embodies the absences as a chronic, undifferentiated emotional hunger."

And we are indeed hungry, hungry for what new products and new entertainments cannot provide. People presumably join recovery groups in order to recover from an addiction—to anything from alcoholism to shopping—or from some blow dealt by a dysfunctional family or relationship. However, many individuals these days are so lonely and isolated that they join recovery groups even when they are not sure what they need to recover from; they simply want support, connection, and just plain company. One of my patients, for example, went to Adult Children of Alcoholics (ACOA) meetings even though her parents did not have a drinking problem.

In short, we are hungry for a nonconsumerist experience of life. We want a taste of something real, something authentic, something that satisfies our deeper longings. In all of us there is a pervasive, nonnegotiable need for a sense of belonging and a set of values that give life meaning.

None of us entirely escapes such hunger. The needs that victimhood attempts to meet are not strange or bizarre; they are quintessentially human. But victimhood does not deliver what it promises, nor do the psychotherapy, recovery, and self-help programs to which some of us turn in search of answers and meaning in our lives. These programs may keep us afloat, but they do not help us swim to shore. Because, as I will explain in the coming chapters, the assumptions of therapy and recovery are borrowed from the very society that has created the "victims," they cannot heal our emotional wounds.

2

....

The Tyranny of Victimhood

In an attempt to find answers to the question "Who am I?" we set about creating and discovering labels that clarify and identify us. For those of us who have yet to settle into a satisfactory identity, a label can be comforting—even a label that defines us in negative terms, such as codependent, alcoholic, or ACOA. We cherish the moment of certainty when we feel we have unlocked the secret of our own character. Unfortunately, by now we have so extensively labeled ourselves that we have limited who we are (and what we can become) and pathologized our personalities.

Every word is a label, in the sense that it is a symbolic representation of some object or event. Ernest Becker, in *The Birth and Death of Meaning*, shares the insight that an infant—a baby who does not yet use language—receives direct feedback from the environment based on his or her bodily functions. The infant cries and the world responds or doesn't respond. Becker points out that from the moment we utter our first words, we will forever be responded to in terms of our language. And since language is only a symbolic representation of the real self, we always live one step removed from direct reality.

This is not to suggest that we return to grunts and groans or silence, but only that we must not mistake symbols, which are so convenient, for the real thing. Words are an objectification of a subjective experience; hence they are only approximations. But that unbridgeable gap between the experience and the verbal, limited representation of that experience has not stopped us from pretending that the label is the reality. For example, we are quick to explain our sister's unhappiness as "empty nest syndrome," as if that label somehow gives it a stronger, more meaningful reality than the simple fact that "she misses the kids."

In Western culture, classifying and labeling are natural things to do. Science is based on identifying and defining objects for the purpose of controlling them. Applied to human beings, this scientific activity operates with the same goal. If we can give it a name, then we can grasp it, manipulate it, control it, make it serve us, or—if it's negative—work on getting rid of it. If a psychologist on "Oprah" declares that feeling insecure about high levels of success is called the "Impostor Phenomenon," then we suddenly feel relieved; the definition implies that our vague sense of insecurity is a phenomenon that once identified can now be eradicated.

In our eagerness to "pin things down," we have sliced and diced and shelved our experiences into such tiny categories that we have nearly forgotten how to simply describe behavior. A fellow writer confided to me that he hesitates even to tell anyone about the struggle of writing for fear that someone—well-meaning, of course—will diagnose it as "writer's block," "code-pendent perfectionism," or "fear of success." Not only do we label our own behaviors and feelings in order to give ourselves an imaginary sense of security, we also label others', and for the same reason.

Terms such as *psychosis, neurosis,* and *alcoholism* are just labels, meaningless in themselves. For example, although you may feel great relief at being able to confess out loud, "My name is Sandy, and I'm an alcoholic," no universal agreement exists on what an alcoholic *is.* Is it someone who drinks more than he or she would like to, or is it someone who can't stop drinking once the first sip is taken? Labels change with the times, too; *melancholia* has pretty well disappeared from the language of treatment, and *introversion* is no longer popular. *Manic/depressive* is now *bipolar.*

No longer are we allowed to have interesting personality quirks or oddities. Psychopathological terms have crept into our every-day language. Casually, we declare that "you're paranoid," "she's anal," or "he's schizy." We are sure that the neighbor who spends hours on his stamp collection is an obsessive/compulsive or the friend who feels moments of great excitement and then is down in the dumps must be bipolar. You cannot risk being eccentric, a rogue, or unusual, or even march to a different drummer, without being thought of as missing some dots on your dominos.

It is not uncommon for us to call an ex-lover "flaky" or a coworker "paranoid," totally unaware that we have not only de-humanized these people, we have also utilized terms that remove us and them from any approximation of reality. The reality is that "My ex's inconsistent behavior frustrates me and makes me angry" or "I feel that my coworker doesn't trust me." Here is where labels become dangerous. They are a cheap attempt to tag people and put them on the shelf. Labeling tends to become an adult version of name-calling. With the help of the "helping professions" as well as self-help and recovery programs, we have turned the name-calling on ourselves as well as others: "I'm an alcoholic" rather than "I drink more than I want to."

Labels are seductive because they are often fun as well as convenient: "Don't cross him; he's a Scorpio" or "You're just like me; you're a 'two' in numerology." People love to talk about the Myers-Briggs Type Indicator, happily classifying themselves and others as "ESTJ" (Extroverted Thinking with Sensing) or "INFP" (Introverted Intuition with Feeling) and figuring out which types get along best together. Such tests and labels make for great cocktail-party conversation, and not only that, they are sometimes useful in helping us understand one another. But although these little labels often contain some morsel of truth, the problem is that we give them too much power. All of us are guilty of being too eager to use labels to classify and objectify ourselves and others. Conveniently labeled, we turn into walking bags of categories, scientific terms, and pathological diagnoses. We are no longer unique, sometimes unpredictable individuals. We are just things. Labels limit our sense of freedom to be whoever we wish to be.

In addition to boxing us in, placing value judgments on what is merely behavior, and depriving us of individuality, labels are bound to disappoint us when we attempt to use them to alleviate emotional pain. Eventually we discover that the labeling is a temporary, wholesale, and illusory concept that has no power at all to reduce suffering.

While labels offer some degree of immediate relief, they also diminish us. We become captured as if on film. Since we initially find labels somewhat reprieving—"Oh, so that's what's wrong with me"—we seek out others who reinforce our labels, a role that therapy and recovery groups are only too happy to fill. In this way labeling oneself a "victim" provides temporary relief at the same time it creates a crippling identity.

Bill is a businessman who began experiencing panic attacks at the age of thirty-one. At first the attacks seemed to come at any time and in any place. Then, as is common, he started to associate the panic attacks with certain places and began to feel comfortable only in the security of his own home. Since he was an outgoing, independent sort of person, this narrowing of his world caused him great anguish.

After being misdiagnosed by several doctors and therapists, he happened to tune into a television program and discovered a term for his condition: agoraphobia. When he found out his problem had a name, he shed tears of joy. "The name made my situation real for the first time and I realized I wasn't crazy after all," he reported to me later. After that, he read many self-help books and took a number of recovery courses. He made much progress but still felt the pain of anticipating a panic attack every time he thought about going somewhere. "What if I get to the restaurant and halfway through the salad my agoraphobia kicks in? What if I lose control and scream or run out of the restaurant? People will think I am crazy."

Bill enrolled in a therapy group I was offering for people with agoraphobia. After the first session he called, wanting to see me for a private meeting. He entered my office in an agitated state and threw a metal object on my desk. "I've decided I'm not going to be an agoraphobic for anybody!" he declared.

I picked up what I immediately recognized to be a medical identification bracelet. "What's this about?" I asked.

"Just look on the back of it," Bill explained. I read on the underside the words "I am an agoraphobic and I may show signs of shaking, sweating, and hyperventilation."

Still upset, Bill went on to explain. "I'm tired of being a phobic. Everything I do I feel it is Bill, the phobic, doing it. It's gotten to the point where I don't know if I'm afraid to go certain places or if I just don't want to go. All my friends now are other phobics. We have a telephone support network, I get four phobia newsletters, I read every new book and article on anxiety, and now I'm in another therapy group. I'm getting sick of telling my story of how anxiety has ruined my life and I'm tired of hearing other people's stories. I'm really scared to think that my whole identity has become defined by my fears. I don't know who Bill is anymore other than Bill the phobic. I've suddenly realized that my anger at having lost my identity is even stronger than the anxiety itself!"

I was quite impressed by Bill's revelation and told him so. I also told him that I have always objected to the use of the terms *phobic* or *agoraphobic* and go out of my way to use the expression "a person with agoraphobia," just as I'd prefer to say "a person with diabetes" rather than "a diabetic" or "a victim of diabetes." I believe that this is not simply a minor linguistic difference. "Agoraphobic" or "victim of agoraphobia" implies a dominant or permanent state, while "someone with agoraphobia" suggests that the condition is only one of an individual's myriad characteristics, and moreover, a condition that can change over time.

Our use of terms like these has an enormous impact on our self-image, as Bill had been wise enough to discern. No label can possibly embrace all the individual differences among those who share in the limited characteristics defined by the label. A psychological label, at best, is a still frame in a very long movie. Still, we often try to keep the "fit" of our labels fitting by gathering in groups to reinforce our identification. Assuming a label, whatever it is, nails our suffering in place. And there is no more crippling label in our society today than that of *victim*.

When Bill threw his medical bracelet on my desk, he was saying, indeed rebelliously proclaiming, that he is "nobody's victim."

A DANGEROUS SOLACE

Both Bill and—less consciously—Nancy experienced the dangerous limitations of declaring themselves victims. But this label contains implications that extend far beyond the personal.

When large segments of the populace fall sway to the allure of victimhood—which certainly seems to be the case in the 1990s—the resulting polarization of victims and perpetrators rends the social fabric. Lashing out at our abusers seems to be the only way of regaining power—sometimes even the only way of getting noticed. Also, retaliation seems an appropriate response to the evil that's been done to us. Powerlessness thus leads to anger, and anger to violence: arguably the number-one social problem in America today. The fear and separateness engendered by this "us versus them" mentality only reinforce the loneliness and sense of isolation that send us searching for a place in the world.

When the anger of the powerless victim does not erupt in outward violence, it is turned inward and reflected in despair.

Deep in the history of our national personality lies the idea that we are invincible. A core assumption about who we are as a society is that we can overcome every adversity. And this image has been bolstered by impressive successes in eradicating disease, beating the bad guys, and triumphing over economic woes. This spirit extends to individuals as well as the nation itself. Triumphing over a physical disability, a person becomes a star athlete; born in poverty, another goes on to make millions. We are so imbued with this success image that we feel guilty and un-American when we cannot bear the weight of our own unique social, economic, political, and psychological realities.

Paradoxically, Americans, who value self-sufficiency and individual success so highly, are becoming more and more willing to settle for the power of powerlessness, i.e., a discovery that being hurt gives you so much needed control and power. Many patients will say, "The only attention or caring I ever got was when I was sick." Since our social world does not satisfy our hunger, we turn, at last, to the suffering itself for meaning.

When we experience life's burdens as overwhelming, it can seem easier simply to withdraw from them, saying, in effect, "If I can't win, I won't play." Developmental psychologists note that a child who is overchallenged—for example, by a toy that is too sophisticated for his or her developmental stage—feels overwhelmed and may retreat into apathy, accompanied by feelings of diminished self-worth and anger. The child may cry, whine, and fuss. She may blame the toy, even kick it. The victimized inner child is apparently quite similar.

It is tempting to feel that life is so worthless and hopeless that there is no point in trying to right social wrongs, or even in attempting to make sense of life's mysteries. Complaining and acting out are easier and, as we have seen, more satisfying in a lot of ways.

Unlike psychotherapy, which assumes that you can gain control over your emotions—and, in fact, that you are responsible for doing so—recovery assumes that someone else is responsible for your suffering, and that control is pretty much impossible. The first of the "twelve steps" is to "admit that we were powerless," and the second deposits control in the lap of a "higher power." After that, the most an alcoholic or addict can do is to exercise a form of mini-control "one day at a time."

I object most of all to this assumption of powerlessness. How can powerless people ever manage to take control of their own lives? How can they ever expect to stop feeling like victims? To assert that an external power can save us is a form of tyranny.

If therapy thrives on reason, recovery veers away from it. *Feelings* are what count—to the point that a recovery program begins to embody a kind of codependency itself.

Both therapy and recovery encourage narcissism. Many sufferers, rather than experiencing the help that these services offer and then moving on with their lives, develop a new persona defined by their problems. At worst, recovery and therapy lock us into our suffering—not only failing to nudge us out of the rut of victimhood, but helping to dig the rut deeper. At best, they "cure" by cutting us off from the world and distracting us from contextual issues. As a result, although they provide moments of insight and comfort, the results from the treatment alone are rarely lasting. Emptiness and hunger remain.

Victimhood not only encourages the "me-versus-myself" attitude (it's all your fault if you feel bad); even worse, it perpetu-ates the "us-versus-them" mindset. Men and women, whites and people of color, especially those who feel they have been abused, often feel that reaching out to one another and finding common ground would compromise their solidarity, give amnesty to the abusing person or group, and sap their political resolve to over-come their victim status.

Declaring victimhood *can* be a useful first step in integrating personal feelings and starting a political movement for change. But ultimately, *remaining* in victimhood helps no one. Alienation prolongs the sense of loss and increases the danger of victimiz-ing others.

ARE YOU STUCK IN THE VICTIM CYCLE?

While some people find genuine solace and support in de-claring themselves victims, many more have a glimmer of its lim-itations. I look at the "victims" who seek my services not in terms of the degree of their perceived abuses, but in terms of their re-sponses to their abuse. Adopting this viewpoint (and aware that I'm treading dangerously near the label trap), I've observed two major categories:

• *Irresponsible victims*—those who use their abuse to gain power and/or avoid taking responsibility. In this category are the Noble Victim, who suffers silently and feels helpless to outgrow his abuse; the Professional Victim, who lets everyone know the hor-rors of her abuse and uses therapy or recovery to create institutionalized witnesses to her suffering; and the Cop-Out Victim, who blots out suffering with medication in order to keep functioning.

• *Responsible victims*—those who are willing to assume responsibility for helping themselves or obtaining help, and who genuinely want to move on.

Those in the latter category would like to give up feeling powerless; they feel unhappy and unfulfilled in the victim role and yearn for a measure of independence. Yet they are afraid to sever ties with therapy or recovery (or both) and stay stuck. One reason is that helpers as well as victims often have unexpressed needs to continue the relationship. Another reason is that the sufferers are unaware—or only marginally aware—of how being stuck in treatment restricts their lives and perpetuates their victim status.

If you feel *you* may be stuck in the victim mode and in the "help" that is attached to it, you would be wise to ask yourself certain probing questions:

- How much time am I spending in recovery programs, reading self-help books, or going to psychotherapy sessions?
- Am I becoming impatient with my fellow group members and starting to feel tired of hearing their stories and my own?
- To what extent do I feel that my work with recovery programs and/or psychotherapy is helping me feel more independent?
- To what extent do I feel that my work with recovery programs and/or psychotherapy is contributing to my dependence?

- How much would I miss my involvement with recovery groups and/or psychotherapy if I were to discontinue it?
- Do I feel guilty when I think about leaving my recovery group and/or psychotherapy? Am I reluctant to stop for fear that others will feel abandoned?
- Have I been able to develop other nonrecovery, nonpsychotherapeutic sources of support in my life?
- When I think about living my life without recovery programs or therapy, how does it feel?

If even contemplating these possibilities fills you with dread, the anguish of self-doubt may be a greater abuse than the abuses that drove you into treatment. Excessive dependence on therapy, recovery, and self-help, like excessive dependence on anything, severely limits your potential and prolongs a sense of helplessness. You partake of treatment but are never fulfilled, because "help" programs offer only a cheap substitute for what is missing in your life. Therapy and support groups cannot replace true community; hired empathizers can never serve as well as caring family members and friends. You must either go outside the victim business to address your real needs or find within it those few practitioners who are not merely extensions of a withholding society.

What would happen if you were able to discard the shackles of life-diminishing assumptions, break the bonds of self-pity, and get on with your life? What if, courageously reaching through the emptiness, you could grasp clarity and empowerment without becoming stuck in professional or peer-group treatment programs?

You would be able to stand up and say, "My suffering is not up to you." You would be nobody's victim.

3

The Limitations of Therapy and Recovery

No psychotherapy's initial claims of remarkable results have stood the test of time and independent investigation.

Bernie Zilbergeld

To understand why you have become mired in recovery or therapy, unable to overcome the victimization that brought you there in the first place, it's important to realize that you have not put yourself there singlehandedly, and that it's not necessarily in everyone's interest for you to move on. Consumers and purveyors of "help," in the form of recovery and psychotherapy, are dance partners. Both are eager to assign labels and identify something that is "abnormal." Therapy and its self-help/recovery offshoots have not only responded to our national victim posture, they have encouraged it, have sometimes helped create it, and certainly have cashed in on it.

As Stanton Peele, author of *The Diseasing of America*, explains:

> The self-exacerbation of addictive problems is closely
> tied to the self-exacerbation of fear. The more we fear a
> problem, the more we worry and warn people about it,
> the more instances of the problem we find and the
> greater our perception of the danger. The process is one
> of a progressive sense of loss of control; the greater the
> number of things we discover to be afraid of, each of
> which individually inspires progressively more fear, the
> more depressed and frightened we become. Indeed, the
> reported incidences of both depression and anxiety are in-
> creasing, just as more people enter treatment for each and
> just as we boast of remarkable breakthroughs in treatment
> for each.

Philip Cushman adds, "Patients with disorders of the self are
empty and hungry for idealizing and merging and thus are in a
highly suggestible and vulnerable state. Their wish to be guided
and taken care of is one that can easily be exploited." Thus demand and supply expand concurrently, feeding on each other.

When any industry grows large, it takes on a life of its own
and begins to require more and more raw material. Therapists,
recovery gurus, and those who prey on twelve-steppers perceive
a potentially rich source of income, as do attorneys who make
their livings representing victims against their victimizers. Is it any
wonder, then, that the past couple of decades have witnessed an
explosion of new forms of victimhood: post-traumatic stress disorder, date rape, codependence, and so forth? Somehow, we got

along without these syndromes before, but now their numbers appear to be limited only by the imagination of those who would treat them or otherwise profit from them.

John Bradshaw, popular author and purveyor of "wounded inner child" workshops, asserts that 96 percent of us come from dysfunctional families. He implies strongly that we are all, therefore, in need of some kind of healing treatment. The marketplace responds to this "need"—sometimes with an excess of enthusiasm.

THE BUSINESS OF TREATMENT

I think most therapists are rather shocked when they leave their training and education programs and realize that psychotherapy is, after all, a business. Graduate school offers no classes on how to market and run a practice. Although most of those who conduct therapy and recovery programs are not exploitive, they have the same need to sell their services and their ideas as anyone else. And the media are eager to help them do so.

Gone are the days when therapists and other healing professionals were not allowed to advertise. Now they can promulgate any message that does not actually promise results or indicate that their program is better than what others have to offer. They can tantalize with such come-ons as "You can learn . . . ," "It's likely that in a few sessions you . . . ," "Clients have reported . . . ," or "Frequently after negative memories or emotions are released . . ."

Author Charles Sykes cites an ad placed by a hospital, urging people to seek treatment for obsessive-compulsive disorder if they can answer yes to *any* of the following questions: Do you avoid using public telephones or restrooms because they might be dirty or "germy"? Are you often late because you have to check things over and over before leaving the house? Do you feel the need to do things symmetrically so that they are "evened up"? Sykes wryly queries, "Has the author of this ad ever *seen* a bus-station bathroom?" He rightly points out, however, that as a marketing tool, the ad is nevertheless effective.

The problems that occupy our minds today, such as discontent with one's job or a feeling of general restlessness, would have caused our ancestors to scratch their heads in puzzlement. But helpers can be too quick to latch on to help seekers' disappointments and discontents and turn them into dysfunctions.

I know from experience that it's not easy to tell a potential client on the phone that you don't really think he needs therapy. Even for the most ethical practitioner rents and professional fees must be paid; it's tempting to think, If this person wants to see me, who am I to say no? Need for business—especially in view of the competition created by an overpopulation of therapists— increases a treatment provider's willingness to see virtually anyone's behavior, feelings, or thoughts as dysfunctional, no matter how ordinary and understandable they are in view of the person's particular life circumstances.

In interviews I'm frequently asked, "Just how can someone determine whether they have a problem and whether they need help?" The response I usually give is, "When the symptoms are interfering with the person's normal functioning, then a problem may exist." The definition of "normal" is up to the patient. I don't think it's my right—or anyone's—to decide when someone needs "curing." Some years ago, a woman called me to say, "I haven't left my house in twenty years." She offered no further comment. "That's very interesting," I replied, "but why did you call me?" After a startled pause, she added, "Oh, I want to be able to go out again but I'm afraid." "Ah," I said, "now I'm interested." I made house calls and eventually she was able to rejoin the outside world.

It's not up to me to judge whether or not somebody who has not left her home in twenty years is pathological and needs treatment. Even if people fit the perfect profile in the *Diagnostic and Statistical Manual* (*DSM*), which defines the various mental disorders, it is a form of disrespect or indeed abuse to tell them that if they act, feel, or think in certain ways, then they are suffering from a particular syndrome and should seek help. (This "hands off" attitude does not apply, of course, to those who are in serious danger of harming themselves or others.)

Yet most mental health professionals, up to their ears in the medical model, are looking to pathologize their patients. They assert that they can define what is normal because normal can be defined objectively; normal is "out there," not within the context of one's own unique being. Psychologist Sid Cormier, in his book *Am I Normal?*, tells us that "one out of every three people in the United States will suffer from an emotional, alcohol-, or drug-abuse problem at some point in their lives." He adds, however, that "most people with psychological problems will never seek help. Could this be because they don't know that they have a problem?" One in three? Has the level of pathology been constant, and are we only just recognizing it? Fortunately for those who "don't know they have a problem," there are plenty of helpers out there to tell them.

The victim business encourages and supports the concept of pathology. For example, the *DSM IV* (*Diagnostic and Statistical Manual, Fourth Edition*) purports to define what a "mental disorder" is—and in fact does exclude from this classification such items as the "expectable response to a particular event, e.g., the death of a loved one." However, the manual's effect has been a widespread pathologizing—for reasons pertaining to the dollar end of treatment.

The *DSM IV* identifies a series of "V codes," defined as a "Supplementary Classification of Factors Influencing Health Status Contact with Health Services." The codes identify such situations as Marital Conflict, Occupational Problem, and Uncomplicated [sic!] Bereavement. Although a therapist could well be helpful to someone who fits one of the V codes, the patient's insurance company may not provide reimbursement. Many insurance companies refuse to pay for services that are not considered "medically necessary."

At this point the therapist confronts an ethical dilemma. All too often she chooses a non–V code diagnosis—for example, "Antisocial Personality Disorder," which is classified as a mental disorder, rather than the V code "Adult Antisocial Behavior"—when insurance pays for the former but not the latter. The diagnosis remains forever on the patient's record.

For in-patient services as well, insurance considerations make the need to pathologize very important. During a short employment at a psychiatric hospital, I was approached by a nurse who told me that she had been asked by the medical staff to speak to me about my patient chart entries. I assumed she was referring to my handwriting, but I was wrong. She told me that I needed to soft-pedal the progress my patients were making and to write more about their difficulties. If an insurance company were to read how well a patient was doing, it would not authorize continued treatment.

The same kind of thinking pertains even in less extreme situations. My friend Hal confessed to me one day that several years ago he had gone to a therapist to help him recover from a bad relationship. "I just needed someone to talk to," he explained. "What I discovered was more than I'd bargained for; it turned out that I had a Dependent Personality Disorder. I stayed in therapy a couple of years after I got over Roberta to work on my disorder. I still struggle with it. I'm too easily hurt by criticism; I feel uncomfortable being alone. I'm a classic case, my therapist said." Although it's possible that Hal may suffer with some extreme and unbearable sensitivity and loneliness, don't we all feel hurt by criticism and sometimes feel the pain of loneliness? Sensitivity to criticism and feeling uncomfortable being alone does not justify a diagnosis of Dependent Personality Disorder.

Because therapy is a business, therapists, sometimes against their own principles, feel pressured to identify—if not discover—disorders to which they then claim some ability to treat. In *The Shrinking of America*, Bernie Zilbergeld explains, "To ensure that no one eludes the therapeutic net, counselors divide life into a number of phases or stages, with new ones being discovered all the time, each with its own requirements, problems, and experts."

WHAT THERAPY AND RECOVERY PROMISE

The emotional health industry not only serves us diagnoses that appear to make treatment necessary, it also tells us that non-

pathological misery can be quickly relieved, and that total fulfillment is possible with the right understanding, behavioral change,
or intellectual insight. Nowhere does therapy mirror our cultural
values more than in the promise of perfecting our lives. Zilbergeld
quotes the goals of therapist Adelaide Bry's "visualization technique":

- To improve the quality of your life in exactly the areas that
  need treatment
- To be healthier, wealthier, and—believe it!—wiser
- To expand your creative talents
- To help you get well when you're sick
- To deepen your feelings of love
- To experience other dimensions of yourself so that you can
  go beyond all your present limitations

Obviously, word of her technique has not gotten around town;
I don't know anybody who has achieved all that.

Given the nearly infinite potential of thoughts, feelings, and
behavior, it is little wonder that new topics pop up all the time
in the victim field: a new form of abuse, a new understanding of
an old problem, or a new breakthrough in treatment. And, like
first-year medical students, laypeople feel that they have developed a case of whatever is going around.

A colleague told me that she took a half-dozen self-evalua-
tion checklist tests in various magazine articles written by psychologists and discovered that she was obsessive-compulsive,
depressed, narcissistic, and mildly voyeuristic. "At first I panicked
and then I thought the panic might be another disorder. I wondered, being the bog of pathologies I must be, how I ever make

it through the day. When I talked to my sister I realized how absurd it was to believe those things about myself. But when I was laughing with another therapist about them, she thought I was in denial."

The minute a natural disaster such as a flood, earthquake, or tornado occurs, therapy experts are on the scene as quickly as reporters, to treat the traumatized victims. Does it make sense to say, "The roof was ripped off my house, my wife's leg is broken, and the cat was killed; can you recommend a good therapist?" Therapists, despite what they imply, have no special magic to make perfectly understandable pain go away.

WHERE THEY FAIL

It is not unusual for people to bounce between the two types of "help"—therapy and recovery—without being able to move beyond victimhood. One type of help seems to offer what the other does not. Yet both are incomplete, in different ways and in similar ways.

Limitations of Therapy

Psychotherapeutic techniques vary widely, as do the skills and sensitivities of therapists, so any characterization of the process must be considered a generalization. Having said this, let me generalize. In psychotherapy, the focus is on the internal construct and process of the individual. The assumption is that early in life—perhaps in infancy or even in the womb—you encountered certain circumstances that, combined with personality characteristics you were born with, shaped your progress through the rest of your existence. Along the way, you internalized others' beliefs and reactions to you—particularly those of your parents. Often, you reacted inappropriately to others and misinterpreted their behavior, with the result that your relationships were less than ideal. You are unhappy, unproductive, dysfunctional, anxious, or whatever because you lack insights and skills. Once you gain these insights and skills, you will be able to control your life and get rid of your emotional pain.

The therapist's job is to apply years of education, training, and professional expertise to identifying the underlying problem—labeling it—and then helping the patient to understand it and/or prescribing behavior-changing assignments or medications. The therapist is like a wise parent, and you are dependent on his knowledge and guidance. On the other hand, you are considered responsible for your own recovery; after all, it is your internal changes that will create improvements, not the behavior of the therapist.

The therapist appears to represent a kind of unattainable goal: having it all together. Therapists do not, as a rule, let patients know about their own personal suffering. Yet they do suffer, as much as their patients do, and they also possess their own quirks and values, which manage to find their way into the therapeutic relationship.

Caring is supposed to be the key to successful therapy, and many therapists do genuinely care for their clients. But since the client must pay for the treatment, a natural dilemma arises. In my experience, patients are keenly aware of this issue, perhaps more than therapists. They clearly need love and concern, but feel confused and distrustful when a charge is levied for it. "What kind of caring is it that stops the minute my insurance runs out?" Such caring feels like a technique rather than a spontaneous emotion.

The noted psychologist Carl Rogers, lecturing to some students, was describing the idea of "unconditional positive regard" when one of the students asked, "At what point in the therapy do you employ it?" Indeed, therapeutic caring resembles just the kind of conditional loving that made patients feel so empty and hurt in the first place that they went into therapy.

Perhaps the dilemma could be resolved by itemizing the therapy bill:

Information	$25
Insight	45
Guidance	10
Honest feedback	15
Sincere caring	no charge

Alas, such billing would hardly serve to fill the patient's valid need for that last item.

Limitations of Recovery

To gain comfort, care, and true understanding from people who have been through the same disabling circumstances, patients turn to peer-support recovery groups. "I don't pay these people, so their caring must be genuine, and they understand my problems because they share them."

In certain recovery programs, modeled after the "twelve steps" of AA, there is no authority figure at all. No parent—just brothers and sisters, fellow travelers on the road toward healing. Other groups are sponsored by recovery gurus (or their lieutenants) and feature exercises and jargon specific to that "expert." But even they do not follow the parent model. They depend on a "We're all in this together" feeling. Learning primarily from one another, members lack an outside perspective and spend a great deal of time reinforcing assumptions of sameness: *unhappy* sameness.

While therapy offers the therapist as an unrealistic, rather distant role model, recovery offers the sponsors—real addicts, just like the new members they advise and watch out for, except that they have usually progressed to the point where their lives are no longer on a downward spiral. It's easier, certainly, to identify with a fellow sufferer than with the superior therapist. However, the sponsors are still taking it one day at a time themselves; they are far from liberated from the shackles of the program. If the role models are themselves dependent people, and the patients' families are dysfunctional, they will find difficulty in forming a picture of what a healthy person looks like.

In short, therapy and recovery are in some ways like opposite phases of the moon. Psychotherapy might be viewed as a sort of "masculine," even macho, system: It emphasizes reasoning, analysis, stoicism, individual responsibility, and restructuring. Recovery, by contrast, is more (what most people would consider) "feminine," with its accent on feeling, nurturing, catharsis, surrender, connectivity, and in some cases religious precepts. As those who have tried therapy *and* recovery have discovered, both are limited by their imbalance, their lack of what the other offers. We need both the masculine and the feminine. We need both connection and autonomy, both acknowledgment of feelings and application of reason. We need empathy and understanding, and at the same time we need to own the reality of our own freedom and responsibility regardless of who did what to whom.

Common Distortions

Beyond incompleteness, therapy and recovery share additional deficiencies:

1. *They look at problems in a mechanistic, linear way, rather than at the whole person.* They categorize and label, creating a new identity for you based on your problems and defined by your pain. Without taking individual differences sufficiently into account, they adopt the view that "if X happened to you, then you will suffer in these ways." They attempt to objectify the subjective. Such formulas that predict the specific unfolding of your emotional pain are forms of disrespect. The loss of your job cannot be described in terms of a research article, "Emotional Consequences of Job Loss." It happened to you; it's your unique, subjective experience. To see you as a victim of the job loss syndrome, sexual discrimination, ageism, or corporate indifference is a form of psychological tyranny that takes *you* out of the equation.

Perhaps the most abusive aspect of some therapy and many recovery programs is the use of "techniques." Practitioners say things in certain prescribed ways in order to elicit particular responses. Any device that is used to control someone's response, even when the motive is pure, is a denial of the person's dignity. Psychotherapeutic techniques may seem innocent in a culture that thrives on creative and technical ways to manipulate and control, but they are superficial at best and degrading at worst. I believe that even if the technique successfully results in a glimmer of insight, it does not justify the violation of your freedom to be in charge of your own process.

Sometimes patients come to therapy and recovery *requesting* techniques—tools that they can use in addressing their problems. In an effort to please these patients, we therapists often scrounge around in our tool chests and end up recommending charts, relaxation tapes, assertiveness training, and other mechanical aids. The human encounter then becomes more like a session in a repair shop. The last thing you need is "salvation" that merely enhances your mechanical skills.

In addition to whatever else they may be, recovery's twelve steps are techniques. There is no room in twelve-step for improvisation; the assumption is that participants need structure desperately and will plunge back into addiction the minute they tamper with or bypass a step in the prescription. I have friends who decided they were drinking more alcohol than they wanted to and have cut down accordingly. If they had gone to AA, they would feel wrong for ever having another single drink the rest of their lives. It may seem helpful to use a program, including a twelve-step, to give you some support in your effort, but it's your life, your drinking issue, and cannot be either characterized or resolved by the arbitrary rules of others.

I think writers write and alcoholics drink. That is, it is an example of the tyranny of labels for people to call themselves alcoholics or even sober alcoholics when they don't drink. How do I know I like pie? Because I'm eating it.

2. In their mechanistic, linear approach, both therapy and recovery fail to consider the totality of your being-in-the-world. Beyond family systems, about which therapists and recovery groups generalize, they tend to ignore the contexts of your social, political, economic, and cultural circumstances. But no one lives in a vacuum. Psychotherapy focuses on your intrinsic, internal workings, and recovery groups usually focus on the people immediately surrounding you. But you are not separate from the myriad, interconnected systems in which you operate. Jungian analyst James Hillman, in the book *We've Had a Hundred Years of Psychotherapy and the World's Getting Worse,* declares: "By removing the soul from the world and not recognizing that the soul is also *in* the world, psychotherapy can't do its job anymore. The buildings are sick, the institutions are sick, the banking system's sick, the schools, the streets—the sickness is out *there.*"

Even with a smaller circle of reference, recovery and psychotherapy limit themselves. Both tend to overlook your physical condition, nutritional patterns, work environment, financial stress, value systems, and response to cloudy days—as if these were not as important as, or as central to, a person's emotional state as an alcoholic mother or a breakup with a lover. A patient once told me that she thought that her husband's allergies affected his temperament. Most therapists would not respond to this by asking the husband, for example, to keep a log of allergic reactions and moods. Therapists too quickly and easily disregard issues that are not within the scope of their education and training.

3. They view problems through specialized lenses, sometimes missing simple explanations. One patient came to me with an inability to write without great difficulty. Her hand would "freeze up" so frequently that she had had to learn how to write with her other hand. She had seen a number of medical doctors, who were unable to make a clear diagnosis and had finally suggested to her that her problem might be psychological. She, too, was convinced, by the time she arrived at my office, that she suffered from an emotional disorder. I duly explored various psychological issues with her, but after several sessions I simply didn't feel that they were severe enough to cause her dysgraphia. Finally, I urged her to seek out another medical specialist, which she did with some reluctance. Indeed, her difficulty turned out to stem from a neurological disorder.

This particular story may make me look good, but I suspect that I have missed as many medical diagnoses as other psychotherapists have. Every treatment professional looks for what he or she has been trained to look for. If someone presents a problem to a specialist in depression, that specialist searches out the signs and warning signals of clinical depression. Similarly, every recovery group focuses on its specialty. The person who comes to an "inner child" workshop is urged to examine the repeated "wounding" visited upon him by parents and others when in fact the source of his unhappiness may be much more immediate.

Individuals encounter the projected values and approaches of each specific therapist or recovery group. The Jungian therapist ends up training her patients to be Jungian. The twelve-step group teaches its members to be perpetual "survivors" (hardly an affirmative label) of a particular kind of abuse. The individual who is re-created in the image of the therapist, the therapist's theory of mental health, or the group's image of an abuse victim/survivor can scarcely feel any more free than he felt in the restrictive circumstances that brought him to therapy or recovery in the first place.

4. Their approaches to healing are based on certain myths and assumptions that do not work in the postmodern world. Among these assumptions, borrowed from the larger society, are the following:

- If you feel bad, you're a victim of yourself or of someone else.
- We all suffer the same.
- Knowing "why" we suffer is essential for recovery.
- We can conquer suffering if we have the character and will to do so.

As a result, therapy and recovery provide the right answers to the wrong questions and the wrong answers to the right questions. For example, if "why?" is the assumed question posed in therapy, then the answer (psychological resolution) leads often to endless analysis, which, in itself, changes nothing in the patient's life.

Recovery and therapy depend on human misery for their livelihood. Letting go is rarely part of their agendas. How can termination of an activity take place when the activity can never complete its promise? As psychiatrist Irvin Yalom points out, even when the therapy is not restricted by the number of sessions, "issues are never resolved once and for all in therapy. Instead, therapist and patient inevitably return again and again to adjust and to reinforce the learning—indeed, for this very reason, psychotherapy has often been dubbed 'cyclotherapy.' " I would like to think that no therapist tries, consciously or unconsciously, to keep a client coming to sessions when the client would be better off leaving, but just as treatment professionals too readily accept patients, they can also be reluctant to let them go. Money may, alas, play a part in this reluctance. Unlike medical practitioners, some of whom keep several examining rooms going at once, the therapist in private practice may struggle to keep a patient load of twenty to thirty per week. If flu season or vacation time hits, or therapeutic termination occurs (that is, the person "gets well" and leaves by mutual agreement with the therapist), then the therapist may experience a serious dip in income. Certainly these factors come into play when a therapist evaluates a patient's readiness to move on.

Therapists also may struggle with their own emotional attachments to certain patients. *Countertransference* is among the labels affixed to this phenomenon. The attachment need not necessarily be personal, however—it may simply be that the therapist has become accustomed to a patient's visit. The habit of seeing Mrs. Holder on Tuesdays at three P.M. will be missed! Every termination feels like a loss, even abandonment, for therapist as well as patient; therapists are not immune to emptiness. Some therapists become attached not only to the patient, but to the process of therapy and their own techniques in particular. "This is working so well—let's see what more we can do with it."

Traditional twelve-step recovery groups are much more upfront than therapists about not letting go. They actually inform members that they will never recover fully—that is, they will always be victims—and will always have to keep coming back. It's true that some twelve-steppers do leave prematurely, denying residual feelings of dependence and proclaiming themselves cured—only to take a greater tumble later on. However, this kind of recidivism is proof not that it is impossible to overcome an addiction, but rather that the recovery group has failed to teach the addict how to survive on his or her own. Faced with a fear of going it alone, without the tools and inner resources that help rebuild their lives, many remain dependent on the program, never really leaving at all. Still hopeless and helpless, they merely trade their addictions to alcohol, gambling, or men who hate women for addictions to the group, the strict format, the sponsor, and the "higher power." They feel unable to take risks, solve problems, or reach out beyond the safe circle of their fellow dependents. Ironically, this sense of dependency is one of the things that made them so miserable in the first place.

5. They offer only limited means of meeting our deep, genuine, quintessentially human needs: acknowledgment, love, self-esteem, security, belonging, connection, and a relief from emptiness. Neither psychotherapy nor recovery can compensate for the lack of meaning and fulfillment that plagues most of us. They are also not equipped to address the larger context of the political and economic system of which we are all a part. They can do nothing more than offer a kind of filler.

For example, Carolyn Shaffer and Kristin Anundsen, authors of *Creating Community Anywhere*, refer to support groups as "protocommunities": associations that resemble true communities but are not as broad or deep or do not last as long. Although twelve-step groups provide safe places to develop openness, trust, listening skills, and mutual support—which are essential to true community-building—these groups are restricted to narrow functions and time slots. Members do not usually know each other's last names. Therefore, it would be a mistake, if what we need is real community, to limit ourselves to a support group only.

Therapy and Recovery's Dependency on Predictability

Many psychiatrists, psychologists, and psychoanalysts would love to believe that their profession is a science, complete with laws that predict human nature. They want to imagine that we can all rely on the percentage of chances that X will lead through Y to Z. But the truths of science do not correspond exactly to the truths of human behavior. Even in the so-called "pure" sciences, an element of surprise exists. In psychology, it's nearly all surprise!

Still, psychological research, fueled by a need to predict and thereby control, continues its attempt to verify direct cause-and-effect relationships in regard to human beings. (In this behavior, it reflects the larger society.) A recent study from the University of North Alabama found that "If you giggle, you are probably highly anxious. If you pull on your hair, you are anxious and have low self-esteem. If you bite your nails, your behavior can be described as obsessive-compulsive, especially if you twitch, too."

I suppose you would be locked up if you giggled while pulling your hair with one hand and biting the nails of the other. I've done some giggling in my life that had nothing to do with anxiety; I suspect most people have.

The desperate attempts by psychological researchers, and their treatment colleagues in therapy and recovery, to formulate systems that identify, categorize, explain, and predict arises from a fundamental assumption that the psyche can be understood using the medical model. When you spend time clearing brush in the presence of poison ivy, the itchy rash you develop later comes as no surprise to you or your dermatologist. Psychologists and recovery groups would take this cause-effect idea further, saying that if you grew up being constantly criticized, you "naturally" would develop low self-esteem. As a result, you would be likely to become a critical mother yourself.

Or perhaps not; not everybody does emulate their parents, after all. Psychologists and others who try to employ the medical model end up saying, often with a surprisingly straight face, "We have found that people react to having had a critical mother in one of three ways: (1) They become critical parents themselves, (2) They become noncritical parents, or (3) They fall somewhere in between." In any case, their behavior was caused by their mothers' behavior.

It is not just in academic research and psychology that this sort of nonsense takes place. Pursuing the myth of human behavior as scientific construct, the majority of recovery book writers and workshop gurus also hold tight to the idea of predictability. In this respect, treatment programs mirror the larger society, which seeks something immutable to hold on to in the face of a rapidly changing, erratic world.

In order for me to try to predict your behavior I must freeze you in time. I can't analyze and control the subject if it's moving around. I must stop your moving and changing; I must stop your process. One of the ways I might try to do this is to slap a label on you: extrovert, obsessive, procrastinator, etc. I can now suspend your personality, like a laboratory specimen, so that I can see how it responds to various manipulations by other variables.

Of course, when the subject is frozen, a viable subject no longer exists. Imagine someone showing you a snapshot of a park in Alaska and saying, "This is Alaska." ("Gee, it's much smaller than I imagined.") A viable subject is one that is in movement and in a context.

The more conscious you are, the more trouble I will have in defining, controlling, and predicting your behavior. If you insist on acting like an evolving, dynamic human being, you're going to make my research more difficult. Freedom contaminates my protocol; it throws a wrench into my five-step program to cure you of nail-biting.

Just as stopping the bank's surveillance tape might help identify the robber, bracketing a portion of an individual's personality or behavior might reveal something interesting. Yet confusing partial still frames with real life as it is actually lived is as dangerous to science as it is to humanity. An attachment to predictability requires ignoring (a) the nearly infinite and unique combination of variables within each person, (b) the nearly infinite and unique interactions of those inner variables with the world, and (c) the reality of self-determination. It boxes people in and treats them as objects lacking individual power, thus perpetuating victimhood. Victims may find themselves caught up in blanket definitions and labels, imposed from outside, that leave little room for individuality and keep them stuck in limited and unfulfilling roles.

When predictability becomes causality, however, it is very difficult to keep the medical model intact. A critical mother cannot cause you to break out in a rash of criticism. Another approach used to justify the medical model is to treat exceptions as aberrations. If you come from an abusive childhood, yet manage to live a life that is stable and fulfilling, you are termed "resilient," implying that you have achieved some kind of abnormal health-against-the-odds. Yet variations, surprises, and unaccountable consequences are the stuff of life, perhaps more "normal" than predictability.

Defenders of psychological science argue that, at least statistically, patterns or tendencies of behavior exist. True enough. But what does that mean to you personally? You might react to your mother in any number of ways, given the nearly infinite number of other variables—including the fact that you are being studied by psychological researchers—that form the totality of your experience.

What's embarrassingly missing in psychological research is the acknowledgment of freedom. Imposing prediction and control on the study of human beings necessitates seeing the individual as an object. However, viewing humans as subjective freedoms totally disrupts the "scientific" agenda, which seeks to categorize even the exceptions that impose themselves between the stimulus and the response. Science fails to take into account the *pause* between stimulus and response in which we can exercise choice. (See chapter 10 for more on this subject.)

WHEN HELP HURTS

Although therapy and recovery often help people cope with emotional problems—at least in the short term—sometimes these programs actually hurt more than they help. For example, violations of the therapeutic relationship through sexual seduction (or even response to sexual seduction by the patient) severely damage many a patient's life. Most researchers feel that the frequency of such sexual encounters is much greater than the one therapist in ten reported (by the therapists themselves) in various surveys. As psychotherapist Laura Markowitz points out, "The very factor that allows treatment to be successful—the power of the therapeutic relationship—is also the very thing that has the potential to do terrible harm."

One particularly dangerous recent phenomenon is the "false memory syndrome," in which patients, encouraged by their therapists or their recovery groups, have suddenly recalled long-buried "memories" of being molested by their parents, other relatives, or trusted friends. In some cases, the memories have included bizarre satanic rituals. The patients accused these identified perpetrators, and in some cases sued them, even a half-century after the recalled incident. As families shattered, many of the accused protested their innocence; a group of anguished parents started the False Memory Syndrome Foundation, from which many thousands of other parents sought help.

Some of the accused, it turned out, *were* innocent. Growing numbers of patients came to the realization that their memories were not memories at all, but figments of overheated imaginations stimulated by therapy. Their anger was then turned upon their therapists. A *San Francisco Examiner* investigative study reported that "therapists are facing an aggressive new wave of lawsuits by former patients who have renounced their 'memories' of incest; by those who say they've been falsely accused of abuse; and now by patients recovering memories of abuse by the therapists themselves." One lawyer predicted a ten-year wave of litigation costing $250 million. (And that was *before* a father who had been accused of abusing his daughter had successfully sued his daughter's therapists for planting false memories—the first lawsuit won by someone other than the patient.)

The question of the validity of recovered memories has split the therapeutic profession. While some professionals denounce recovered-memory therapy as the greatest scam of the century, others just as heatedly defend it, accusing detractors of denial and of creating a backlash against survivors of incest and child abuse. The American Psychological Association set up a task force to investigate the issue, and the American Medical Association warned that popular memory-inducing techniques such as hypnosis, guided imagery, and body massage were "fraught with problems of potential misapplication."

It was clear that at least some overeager therapists had shot themselves in the foot. The great irony, of course, is that they had also created new business for other therapists who were then called upon to treat the victims of dysfunctional therapy.

Statistics on therapy's less than perfect "success" rate abound. A study by psychologist Allen Bergin of Brigham Young University, covering a broad range of therapeutic schools, concluded that 5 to 10 percent of patients were actually worse after treatment. A later study by Professor Alan Gurman of the University of Washington reported similar rates of deterioration after family therapy. Of course, in view of the many factors operating in a client's life, it is difficult to determine cause and effect.

Bernie Zilbergeld describes a study comparing groups of clients who received behavior therapy, psychoanalytically oriented psychotherapy, or no formal counseling at all. The study found that "93 percent of the behavior therapy clients and 77 percent of the psychotherapy clients improved on a measure of overall adjustment. This looks incredibly impressive until you know that 77 percent of the control group also improved on this measure."

With support groups, measuring success is even more difficult. Since many traditional recovery groups welcome drop-ins, and many participants attend meetings of more than one group, there is little continuity. One highly dysfunctional member can destroy a group, but this is not necessarily life-shattering for the other members, who can usually move on to different groups. There are no professional review boards to monitor peer-based recovery associations and "self-help" workshops to ensure ethical behavior.

In psychotherapy, the potential for harm always exists, as evidenced by therapists' heated wrangling over certain approaches. How distant should therapists be from their patients—for example, should hugging be allowed, or is that an egregious violation of the client's boundaries? Are "dual relationships"—e.g., friend or colleague in addition to client/therapist—dangerous to the patient? What kind of confrontation should be employed, and when? Should therapists take an eclectic approach, using techniques from various schools according to the perceived needs of the patient, or should they specialize? Is it asking too much for a therapist to know what theory or technique to apply at any particular moment on another infinitely mysterious human being?

In an *Atlantic Monthly* article entitled "The Wounded Healer," author Thomas Maeder suggests that the very fact that a person chooses psychotherapy as a profession indicates that he is likely to be, if not actually unstable, at least somewhat pathological. "Such people may be lured, knowingly or unknowingly, by the position of authority, by the dependence of others, by the image of benevolence, by the promise of adulation, or by a hope of vicariously helping themselves through helping others." Secondary "less-than-selfless motives" may include "sublimated sexual curiosity, aggression, the problem-solving pleasure of clarifying emotional confusions, and a voyeuristic interest in the lives of others." He cites a number of studies to bolster his points, including one revealing that psychiatrists kill themselves about twice as often as other physicians.

Even those rare and wonderful therapists who are not emotionally unbalanced are, nevertheless, human. Unfortunately, patients *want* to see these people as experts who possess the answers that they themselves lack. They are eager to buy into any pretense of omnipotence. "Cure me," is the implicit plea, and the therapist may begin to feel that she is not doing her job if she doesn't maintain the image of a total healer. *Cure,* a term adopted from the medical model, suggests that pain can be eradicated. Yet recovering from the loss of a child is not the same as healing a broken arm. Therapy and recovery are not panaceas—life is too complicated—and remaining in treatment too long can solidify a sense of dependence and powerlessness.

To find healthier, more effective approaches to meeting your basic needs—approaches that make the role of victim, and the wheel-spinning in therapy and recovery, unnecessary—you need to take a hard look at the assumptions of treatment and "healing" programs. If you don't question these assumptions, it can be all too easy for you to become trapped in a system that is supposed to set you free.

4

....

Tools of the Trade:
The Methodology of Therapy
and Recovery

Nancy, the self-confessed "therapy junkie" I discussed earlier, experimented with every type of treatment she could find. Each seemed like the "right" answer at first because it provided a focus that the previous one had lacked. During our first session I asked her to tell me a little about her therapeutic history. She jumped at the opportunity.

My first shrink was Freudian, and I spent four days a week trying to uncover the real reason for my misery. To help me survive during my treatment he gave me antidepressants. I don't know if it was the antidepressants or the analysis, but I just felt worse and worse about myself. And it was taking so much time—therapy was becoming my life!

After three years I'd had enough, so I started seeing a behavioral therapist. She told me that insight wouldn't help and that I just needed to take action. She would give me homework assignments such as exercising and becoming more assertive with people. I started feeling good enough to get off the antidepressants, but I still felt something was wrong or missing. I didn't feel like a whole person.

When I felt that I'd gotten all I could get from behavioral therapy, I started reading the new books on cognitive therapy: Changing your thinking changes your feelings. I saw a cognitive therapist for two years. He tried to correct, or reframe as he called it, so much of my thinking that I began to doubt everything I thought. I finally had to break away.

Although her therapy had not healed her distress, Nancy could not be faulted for failing to search. She had endured various forms of the two main types of therapeutic treatment:

- Those that focus on understanding the historical causes of emotional pain (insight therapy)
- Those that focus on treating the symptoms of emotional pain (e.g., behavioral and cognitive therapy).

She had also participated in support groups, which by and large fall into the second category, as we shall see below. *Both approaches, which reflect the cultural attitudes of the time, leave out some essential ingredients that allow people to move beyond victimhood.*

The "Logic" of Insight

I knew my colleague Winston was becoming burned out when he told me at lunch, "At this point I wish everyone would just suppress and repress as much as possible." He suddenly looked nervous, as though this heretical statement had just excommunicated him from the helping profession.

"I sometimes feel the same way," I reassured him.

Encouraged, he continued, "I spend my whole life reflecting! I invite my patients to reflect on their feelings, then I reflect on their feelings and behavior, then I reflect on how I feel about their reflections. Sometimes I wonder if I've lost the ability to just be—to feel and act without analyzing. Then I start reflecting on why I feel that way. Am I avoiding something? I often feel overwhelmed by the endless onslaught of psychology books—it's like another load of sand to be counted."

Perhaps Winston just needs to take some time off or join a rock band to get some diversity into his life. Or maybe he's trying too hard to get his patients to delve into the causes of their problems. The stress of trying to figure out someone (much less dozens of patients) can be debilitating. Can it be that the very activity of analyzing is a flaw in the profession itself?

Here I'm using the term *analyze* in its generic meaning, not in reference to specific schools of psychology such as Freudian psychoanalysis or Jungian analysis—although insight therapy does derive directly from the theory of the unconscious. Regardless of their theoretical orientations, many therapists feel it's their job to interpret their patients' feelings, thoughts, and behaviors. The old cliché that therapists have to hear from time to time, "I better watch it—you're probably going to analyze me!" arises from the long traditional therapeutic emphasis on figuring out, interpreting, and understanding, at deeper and deeper levels.

To an insight therapist, understanding is the heart of cure—in fact, it amounts to cure. Misery arises from lack of knowledge. Once you understand what lies beneath your behavior, the behavior will modify itself. Often it is the therapist who must understand first, then lead the patient to a similar understanding. Once the therapist has discovered what makes you tick, he or she can help you see it yourself, and once you do, you're on the road to mental health. You do need to pave the road, though. The therapist makes it clear that your suffering is your own personal issue and that any success depends solely on your inner exploration.

In any case, the therapist acts as a kind of macho miner who shines a light behind you as you descend into the cave of your unconscious. Until you excavate and retrieve the jewels of insight from your unconscious, you will never really be able to trust your thoughts, feelings, or actions. You are seduced into feeling guilty if you don't want to go down into the cave, and you are never really satisfied when you bring your treasure to light because there is always more. Even when you attempt to leave therapy, the therapist often insists that there is yet another rich vein of truth that must be explored.

Burrowing further and further into the psyche in a relentless search for the "cause," an insight therapist will help you take yourself apart as though you were an automobile engine. According to my American Heritage Dictionary, analysis is "the separation of an intellectual or substantial whole into its constituent parts for individual study." No systems orientation here; you are not a dynamic being-in-the-world, a person in process, but a collection of separate, distinct, and static elements to be examined one at a time. Insight therapy depends on linear thinking and logic.

This exercise of analyzing and figuring out the causes for suffering exemplifies our illusion of our separateness from the world. And it is just this separateness that causes suffering and creates "victims." We suffer because we see ourselves as isolated, cut off. Analysis keeps us tied to the individual self because it creates a closed system, leaving out the universal self. It turns on itself and distorts the direction of consciousness. The deeper analysis goes, the more narcissistic it gets, and this narcissism, focusing so intensely on the intrapersonal at the expense of relationship and connection, feeds victimhood.

In its linear approach to discovering "inner truths," analysis often misses the point. For example, insight therapists (as well as other types of therapists, for that matter) never see political or societal issues as the "cause." If they did, they would claim, with some justification, that they are not in a position to change society, or even to do anything about that particular aspect of society that is causing you pain. Their job, as they define it, is to find out what it is *inside* you that is interacting with society in such a way that suffering occurs. This is almost like blaming the victim. And as we've seen, it's a short step from determining cause to determining blame.

Moreover, what the therapist sees as the cause may or may not have much to do with your pain. The therapist, trained to look for certain factors, brings her particular biases to the process. Whatever doesn't fit her theories is pushed and twisted into a shape that *will* fit, or is ignored. For example, if an "analyst" in the traditional sense of "psychoanalyst" is of a classical Freudian bent, he may not believe that you have been sexually abused, even if you know you have been. He is, at least, bound to consider the *probability* that the abuse is a fantasy, and to look for evidence that supports this theory. From there he moves toward analyzing the unconscious desires that prompted the so-called fantasy.

Jeffrey Masson, author of *Against Therapy*, points out that "the term 'insight' was first used in German psychiatry, where the expression was *Krankheitseinsicht,* which refers to the patient's recognition of his or her own illness. When a patient said, 'I am sick,' he or she was considered to have improved. In other words, a cure was begun as soon as society's definition of illness was accepted personally." (Masson, it should be noted, makes no secret of his conviction that all forms of therapy are dangerous and abusive and ought to be done away with; while I do not share this extreme view, I do agree with many of his points.)

Therapy pretends to provide an objective setting for examining and dealing with pain. But how can it be objective? You don't tell your therapist everything—in fifty minutes there's hardly time to convey the entire context of your week, much less your life— and what you do tell comes out a little at a time, so the therapist can never be fully informed. Every new tidbit you reveal gets filed away in a file that your therapist has already created and labeled. The idea that the therapist knows you is a delusion. Your own priorities and perspectives may be quite different from the therapist's. As Masson comments, "One person's insight is another's nonsense."

Self-analysis, and even more so the analysis of another, is ultimately doomed to failure because the analyzer cannot help using a distorted lens. When you look at someone you've known for thirty years, you see him in terms of that history; he's not simply a man named Lyle, he's *your* Lyle. But when Lyle looks at himself, he sees *his* Lyle. His wife sees hers, and so forth. Moreover, each individual's perception of Lyle changes somewhat as events, and Lyle's responses to them, evolve.

The central question in insight therapy is "Why?" These "why" questions can snag you into an endless cycle of self-reflection, especially if they imply that the answer is, to some extent, an indication of pathology. For example:

"Why do you think you're so hostile?"

"Why are you unable to make a deep commitment to someone?"

"Why do you think you can control your drinking?"

The assumption is that you can't make a deep commitment because of some emotional damage that needs to be identified and analyzed. But there may be a nonpathological explanation: Maybe you haven't made a deep commitment because you haven't met the right person yet, and you're not a romantic fool. And maybe you think you can drink a little because you believe in your capacity to be in charge of your life. You need to be on your toes to avoid the manipulation implicit in "why" questions.

Sometimes the "Why?" is very subtle. For example, a therapist may comment, "I notice you're always late," and then pause meaningfully. The implication is, "You need to figure out *why* you're always late."

Insight—especially making connections between past experiences and present suffering—can provide a certain initial satisfaction. Identifying a cause, if not *the* cause, of your current suffering reduces the feeling of uncertainty. But it goes only partway toward healing. Here's a typical scenario—a composite of several cases I've seen:

Janine entered therapy six years ago because she felt immobilized by depression. Her therapist has a thick file full of information and interpretive insights about Janine's family and upbringing. During their sessions, Janine reflects on her family and the therapist offers possible explanations that link her reflections to her present state of mind. Although she is less depressed than she was before starting therapy, it's probably because of the caring attention she receives from her therapist, rather than the intellectual insight she has developed. Her therapist has devoted no attention to other issues in Janine's life, and has not suggested any steps that she might take to put her insights to use in her current relationships or work. He has assumed that her suffering diminishes as a function of the quality of his insightful explications.

Insight therapy is based on the idea that answering the question "Why?" is enough. It does not ask "What next?" Anne Wilson Schaef, author of *Beyond Therapy, Beyond Science,* declares, "I believe that no one has ever healed in his or her logical mind. No one has ever healed from 'understanding' something. Yet much of our psychotherapy is built on the belief that if we just *understand* something, we will be all right."

One key difference between us and the lower animals, some say, is that we are able to reflect. When a monkey misses a vine and falls on his behind, he does not ask "Why?" He may instinctively change the way he leaps next time, but he does not review and reflect, as we would do. We are not just aware; we are aware of our awareness. While reflection is the unique way humans have of reassessing a troubling situation, overdoing it—reflecting on every act, feeling, and thought—turns a valuable function into a burdensome nuisance. After all, having a good time, feeling love, and enjoying moments of spontaneity are not acts of reflection. Joy is possible only in the nonreflective mode.

Self-reflection is a uniquely human capacity that has become almost too common, addicting even, in today's society. We never trust ourselves these days; we're always second-guessing our thoughts, feelings, and motives, always rehearsing. In my own life I swing between a thirst for deep understanding of my psychic life and a feeling of embarrassment about self-reflection as too self-indulgent and unspontaneous. One day as I was driving along, deep in introspection, I suddenly wondered, Does God reflect? If so, what purpose would such reflection serve? If God does not reflect, then why do *we* spend so much time on it? As a self-aware person, I knew it was time to stop reflecting and just drive.

"Forget Insight; Just *Do* It"

Americans increasingly possess a bottom-line mentality. Pressured by the quickening pace of daily life, we don't like wasting time just talking; we want to take action. We are a nation of doers—just shut up and get on with it! Results are what's important and you don't get results sitting around talking. It is little wonder, then, that this country has seen a shift in the last thirty years toward therapies that attack our symptoms rather than exploring the endless depths of the psyche.

These days, only a handful of therapists see clients for years. Titles of recent books are revealing: *The Twenty Minute Counselor* and *Five Minute Phobia Cure*. We don't just want a fix, involving as little talk as possible, we want a *quick* fix, the magic bullet. "How many sessions will it take to get rid of this problem?" a therapy-seeking caller may ask, or "What is your cure rate?" Such questions assume that the caller suffers from some bug and that the science of psychology should be able to zap it with dispatch.

Two major schools have evolved to meet the public's demand for more down-to-earth and less time-consuming approaches to relieving emotional pain: cognitive and behavioral. While some insight therapists incorporate these approaches into their practice, a strict cognitive or behavioral therapist cares very little about underlying causes. By and large, these practitioners do not deny the existence of historical life experiences, including traumas, that may have contributed to the current problem, but they believe that these causal factors are irrelevant to treatment. They treat symptoms, not causes.

Cognitive therapy is based on the idea that changing your thinking will lead to changes in your emotional state. It asserts that your feelings are a consequence of your thoughts. Although you can't easily and directly change your feelings, you *can* change your thoughts and thereby control your feelings: It's mind over matter.

Cognitive therapist Aaron Beck, author of *Anxiety Disorders and Phobias*, states, "When there is a disturbance in this central mechanism of cognition, there is a consequent disturbance in feeling and behavior . . . our cognitive perspective posits that correction of a disturbance in thinking will relieve disturbances in feeling and behavior."

FIGURE 4-1. DIFFERENCES BETWEEN INSIGHT AND COGNITIVE-BEHAVIORAL THERAPIES

INSIGHT	COGNITIVE/BEHAVIORAL
Analyzing decreases pain	Changing thinking and/or behavior eliminates symptoms
Changes in thinking and behavior automatic once we understand cause	Cause unimportant
Feelings respected but not important to healing	Feelings get in the way of healing; must be conquered
Can take years of work	Brief but hard work

This is about as mechanistic as therapy gets. In effect, it says that you should not dwell on feelings but simply overpower them and control them by using your mind. You suffer because you have learned distorted ways of thinking and behaving, and you need to unlearn them in order to disconnect yourself from your past. Only then will you feel better.

Behavioral therapy concerns itself with what you do rather than what you think. The authors of *BT*, Spencer A. Rathus and Jeffrey S. Nevid, explain that "BT [behavioral therapy] usually begins and ends with focusing on the problem behaviors themselves. BT is the scientific application of the principles of learning to help clients change problem behaviors. BT strategies help you to replace unwanted, troublesome behaviors with desirable constructive behaviors."

I have spent most of my career as a specialist in the treatment of what the field of psychology terms "anxiety disorders." During and after my training, behavioral desensitization and cognitive therapy have dominated the approaches to treating these conditions. (Biopsychiatry, the use of medications, has become a popular treatment as well, and it also ignores insight into cause.) These symptomatic treatments operate as a "war on anxiety," something to be controlled and conquered.

For example, if you have a fear of dogs, you can be exposed to them gradually so as to desensitize yourself. In another, less popular approach, you may be exposed to the most fearful situation—such as being placed in a room full of German shepherds for an hour at a time—with the idea that once you survive the worst possible encounter, your phobia will disappear. (This approach, called "flooding," works only if you experience relaxation before leaving the situation. If you're anxious the whole hour, you'll leave with a reinforcement of the fear rather than being desensitized. This—complete with the German shepherds—actually happened to a patient of mine, before I met him.)

Whether gradual desensitization or flooding is used, behavioral therapists are not much interested in how you came to be afraid of dogs. The fact that a pit bull bit you when you were six years old is irrelevant. I have always been uncomfortable with this one-sided approach.

Some therapists are purely cognitive *or* behavioral, while others refer to themselves as cognitive/behavioral therapists. All operate under the assumption that you can consciously and rationally make changes that will heal your problem or your pain, without spending time trying to understand it. While insight therapy places a high value on feelings, and sees them as important signals of significant issues, cognitive therapy implies that painful feelings are not valuable in themselves. The aim of therapy, in fact, is to eradicate them as quickly as possible. It is not necessary to identify and work through underlying issues in order for healing to occur. In fact, say the cognitive/behaviorists, such analysis will only delay healing.

Sometimes cognitive and behavioral therapy do help relieve symptoms more quickly than talk or insight therapy, especially when the symptoms are not severe. But they shamelessly disregard the rich and powerful feelings that are part of the self.

During my internship I was watching my supervisor through a one-way mirror as she worked with a patient. The patient was distraught over the sudden deaths of her husband and daughter in a car accident. The therapist was comforting, present, and sympathetic. In the last part of the session she recommended some homework: She told her patient to repeat certain affirmations three times a day and to jog three times a week. The patient, head down, was quiet for a long time and then asked plaintively, "But what am I going to do?" The therapist said, "Let me go over the homework assignment again so you know what it is." The patient replied, "I understand about the affirmations and the jogging, but what am I going to do?"

It was a chilling moment. The patient meant, "How am I going to be? I am empty, I've lost my soul, and you want me to go jogging?" I never forgot this experience; its mechanical superficiality offends me. Training people to think and act differently is not the same as healing. It's like painting rust.

Recovery's Approach

Many recovery programs, especially the ones based on the twelve-step program, have adopted a form of cognitive/behavioral theory. AA, for example, offers a set of prescriptions for cognitive and behavioral change. Its twelve steps are:

1. We admit we were powerless over alcohol and that our lives had become unmanageable.
2. We came to believe that a power greater than ourselves could restore us.
3. We made a decision to turn our will and our lives over to the care of God (as we understand God).
4. We made a searching and fearless inventory of ourselves.
5. We admitted to God, to ourselves, and to another human being the nature of our problem.
6. We were entirely ready to have God remove these defects of character.
7. We humbly asked God to remove our shortcomings.
8. We made a list of all people we had harmed and were willing to make amends to them all.
9. We made direct amends to these people whenever possible except when to do so would injure them or others.

10. We continued to take a personal inventory and when we were wrong we promptly admitted it.
11. We sought through prayer and meditation to improve our own contact with God (as we understand God), praying only for knowledge of God's will for us and the power to carry it out.
12. Having had a spiritual awakening as the result of these steps, we tried to carry this message to other alcoholics and to practice these principles in our daily activities.

A thoughtful examination of this list reveals that steps 1, 2, 3, 6, 7, and 11 take a cognitive approach, while steps 4, 5, 8, 9, 10, and 12 take a behavioral approach. Insight is not involved. You do not need to know why you are an alcoholic in order to stop being one.

Support groups generally assume that the cause of your problem or suffering is already known: It was your dysfunctional family, your abusive spouse, your shopaholism gene—it doesn't matter. A logical, rational, step-by-step methodology will eliminate the problem for just about anybody who follows it faithfully. And symptom-treating therapies *do* appear to "work" effectively; for anxiety, they claim success rates upward of 85 percent. However, their claimed success rate is based on observable behavior, not on how someone feels inside.

Cognitive and behavioral therapies, as well as support groups, generally take the narrowest view, treating just one isolated symptom of emotional pain. This one symptom, be it alcoholism, anxiety, or whatever, is assumed to be your Problem, as though all other problems were not only insignificant but unrelated to this

Problem. It's a lot cleaner and simpler this way, and it certainly saves time. Too bad life itself isn't clean, simple, and one-dimensional.

While insight therapy, with its focus on the intrapersonal, reinforces a sense of separateness from others and from the world as a whole, symptom-treating therapies emphasize disconnection of the past from the present, the rational mind from the emotions, behavior from memory and desire, aware-ness from action. It is my firm belief that disconnection of both types is itself dysfunctional. It lies at the root of me-against-myself (it's all your fault) and them-against-me (it's all their fault)—the victim positions.

Taken to extremes, both insight therapy and quick-fix "Mc-Therapy" can be harmful. The former can require you to reflect and analyze four times a week for twenty years, and the latter can discount your history and wipe out your feelings by means of practical actions. The recovery philosophy operates on the level of eliminating symptoms. With support from fellow addicts and a practical checklist of actions, recovery programs see little value in "working through" emotional baggage. Recovery is in the do-ing, not in the resolution of causal issues. In this regard recovery programs are more akin to cognitive and behavioral principles.

I believe that it's not healing either to overanalyze or to over-simplify, to probe endlessly into causes or to simply eradicate a symptom. Even a combination of these approaches still leaves out a great deal that could help you move out of the victim mode.

BREAKING FREE OF THE VICTIM TRAP

....

5

....

Step 1: Owning Your Pain

The first step in shedding your feelings of victimhood is to work toward becoming a responsible victim, as defined on page 26. When we are irresponsible victims we use our abuse for some secondary gain and therefore have little incentive to move on. Only responsible victims have the freedom to de-victimize themselves. For both abusers and abusees, the challenge is the same: awareness and recognizing responsibility. Just like the abusers themselves, if we are not aware of our behavior, there can be no resolution.

The victim business thrives on a certain basic myth: **If you feel bad, there's something wrong with you or with someone close to you**. This "blaming" myth ought to be questioned in therapy and in recovery, but seldom is.

Sheila had shopped at the same local supermarket since she moved to town twelve years before. One day she went to the market when it was quite crowded. Although nothing else seemed out of the ordinary, while standing in the checkout line she began to feel warm all over. A strange, shaky sensation moved through her body, and she began to perspire profusely. Her heart pounded and she started to have trouble breathing. The people in front of her seemed to be taking forever, and she felt like screaming or running from the store. Abandoning her groceries, somehow Sheila managed to leave the line and make it home. To her, the experience was as frightening as dying or going crazy.

She hurried to her medical doctor, but when a complete battery of tests revealed no organic cause, she felt even worse. Now her experience was unexplained, without cause. Since Sheila could identify no rational external cause, and no medical cause could be found either, her mind created one. It said, "It's too scary not knowing what caused this terror, so let's assume it's the grocery store itself; then by avoiding this 'cause' you'll avoid panic attacks." From then on, she steered clear of supermarkets and other places where there might be crowds. Thus a single panic attack escalated into a phobia.

Such a reaction indicates how far our minds will go to assign an external cause to emotional pain, and it is a pattern I see over and over again. As Stanford psychiatrist Irvin Yalom puts it: "If we can transform a fear of nothing to a fear of something, we can mount some self-protective campaign—that is, we can either avoid the thing we fear, seek allies against it, develop magical rituals to placate it, or plan a systematic campaign to detoxify it." The unknown freaks us out; if we can pinpoint a cause, we at least feel that there is some possibility of doing something about it. We can't fight ghosts. We feel we need something—or someone—to blame for our unhappiness.

WHO'S DOING WHAT TO WHOM?

Irresponsible sufferers are especially susceptible to the attractions of affixing blame, as discussed in chapter 2. If the cause involves a person—themselves or, more frequently, someone else—that person becomes a focus for faultfinding. Rather than saying, for example, "My insecurity comes, in large part, as a reaction to my father's cold distance," they declare, "My father has ruined my life and made me insecure."

"Responsible" victims, who want to escape victimhood, often seek help in therapy or recovery. Treatment programs offer two (one or both) explanations for your affliction:

1. Other people have made you suffer.
2. It's *your* fault; something's wrong with you.

These analyses appear to offer resolution, but in fact they usually reinforce your victimhood.

One evening as I sat with a group of friends chatting around the table, the subject of sexism raised its ugly head. At one point in the conversation, Cynthia said that she had recently seen the movie version of *My Fair Lady* and had been appalled by the way it portrayed women. "I was so angry I left the theater!" she declared vehemently.

I must admit that my jaw nearly dropped. "It was only a movie," I finally ventured.

"Yes," she darted back, "but it's that kind of junk that reinforces society's attitude toward women."

"It's only a movie," I repeated, adding, "It's just a portrait of how things were then. It's history, not a training film!"

The other women present were as puzzled as I was, and I know that at least one of them had really loved *My Fair Lady*. Obviously, the same circumstance that creates joy in one person can instill in another a feeling of being victimized.

Are you a victim of what others do to you? This issue lies at the heart of the attitudes about what some critics refer to as a "culture of whiners and blamers." The comments on each side reveal how ambivalent we are about the issue. We feel compassion for those who seem to be suffering, yet simultaneously feel impatient or disgusted by what we believe is a lack of effort on their part to help themselves. Upon seeing a homeless person, your first reaction may be sadness, but when the person approaches you for a handout, you may think, Why should I help you when you won't even help yourself?

This ambivalence extends up through our legal system. There is nothing we dislike more than a state of subjectivity, and we find great security in labels or "objective truth." Yet objectivity is hard to come by. As specifically and clearly as we write the law, the concept of "justice with mercy" muddies it. Juries split and the public feels confused, unable to put the ambivalence away. The written law says, "If you did the crime, you do the time." But justice with mercy is messy, and some people think it creates a mollycoddling loophole: "My friends on the jury, Lorena's abuse at the hands of her husband would have led any reasonable person to sever her husband's penis."

The Menendez brothers, Lyle and Erik, murdered their parents and sought absolution from the jury on the grounds that the parents had physically and mentally abused them for years. Arguments, in and out of court, raged: "You have to feel sympathy for kids who were treated like that." "That's no excuse. They could have gone to authorities about the abuse." "But abused people, especially children, aren't able to do that. Abuse is almost always done in private and there are no witnesses and they'd be powerless against the parents' revenge if they pressed charges." "Well, who were the greater victims, the parents or the sons?"

Certainly it is difficult to dislodge the idea that, even in cases involving the most horrendous deprivations and abuses, the perpetrator might not have had totally free choice—suppose, for example, he was so severely abused himself as a child that he had no model for nonabusive relationships—and the victim might have some degree of accountability. Lack of an objective standard leaves us confused and fuels the legal business.

Author Fritjof Capra tells of tribes in Zaire who bring an emotionally suffering member before the whole community and ask, "What is wrong with us that this man is suffering in this way?" Our society, lacking a concept of group responsibility and interrelatedness, instead needs to point fingers at individuals.

It's a relief to blame your suffering on the acts of others or on a disease. Recovery groups are not only sympathetic, they can't imagine why you wouldn't be suffering given the way you were treated or the genes you inherited. But in relieving you of blame, they are also depriving you of the power to change your situation.

Alcoholics Anonymous is unique in many ways, one of which is that it defines the sufferer's problem as an organic disease, yet prescribes no medical treatment. Defining alcoholism as a disease blames the genes: It's not your fault. You were born with cells that lust for Jack Daniel's. It takes away self-blame and guilt, as well as your total responsibility for recovery: Your genes did it and *you* can't fix it. You are helplessly stuck between your lower power (wino cells) and a higher power that will, if you surrender to it, carry your banner into battle against the lower one. There's no point in taking full responsibility or in struggling to overcome anything, because either way it's out of your hands.

"Look what happened to me!" the victim mired in recovery wails to the group. The group does encourage her to take steps to coddle the inner child or to make amends for past misdeeds, but not to stop being a victim. Once a victim, always a victim, according to recovery.

Biomedical approaches to treatment similarly employ the disease metaphor. They tend to cast blame on "biochemical imbalance," an approach that rests on extremely shaky assumptions. Psychobiological research attempts to establish causal relationships between biochemistry and emotion. Because certain medications taken by certain patients make them feel better, researchers conclude that the drug corrects the chemical imbalance that was causing the misery. This is like claiming that since you feel more relaxed after drinking gin, it's evidence that you were gin-deficient.

Such research sounds serious and important. A presentation at a recent conference of the Anxiety Disorders Association of America was entitled "Increased Regional Blood Flow and Benzodiazepine Receptor Density in Right Prefrontal Cortex in Patients with Panic Disorder." Interestingly, however, many patients recover from panic and anxiety using nonmedical treatments such as behavior modification, breathing, or divorce without doing anything to their "receptor densities."

Is It All Your Fault?

More painful than feeling abused by others is the feeling that somehow you suffer at your own hands—that it's all your own fault. Although therapy does trace many disorders back to parental behavior, its assumption is that regardless of whatever happened to you or is happening to you, your inability to resolve your feelings about it is your real problem. The emphasis is on how you are dealing with the particular event or events. Therapy implies that if you just had enough insight, psychological tools, ability to rise above your resistance, or courage, you would not suffer from abuse.

It's not that therapists are never warm and supportive. They simply tend to see their patients' suffering as an intrapsychic matter for which the patient must accept responsibility. If you're feeling like a victim, they may convince you that you've victimized yourself through wrong responses or "letting it happen." Or that you unconsciously wanted the bad thing to happen. Or maybe you even *imagined* that the bad thing happened when it really didn't. In any event, you need to "work on yourself."

Peggy had had two short-term relationships that involved physical and emotional abuse. She had been in therapy for many years trying to understand why she unconsciously chose abusive men. Feeling that she was getting nowhere with this issue, she decided to see a new therapist: me. I discovered that she had had several other long-term relationships with men who were not abusive and would have married one of them had he not been killed in a car accident. It was clear to me that Peggy was innocent of any charge that she secretly sought abuse. Abusers are often remarkably wonderful people when they are not actually abusing. It is a departure from standard therapy to suggest that she might be guilty of nothing more than two relationships that were abusive, involving men who were abused as children and in turn abused her. Since she could not compute these abusers' behavior, especially since they were also very loving to her, she assumed there was something wrong with her. "How could the person I love treat me this way? I must try harder." Peggy's response to this awareness eventually eliminated the guilt she and her previous therapist had imposed on her.

As a friend told me, "It's not as though a woman has to go out of her way to find an abusive man—they're everywhere!" Whether we agree with this dismal assessment or not, I think there is very little evidence in most cases for pathological selection of abusers. When we assume some deep, dark, unconscious motive, it is not difficult to come up with some story to support it. As the Yiddish proverb says, "If you want to beat a dog, you can always find a stick."

Sometimes the therapeutic relationship focuses *entirely* on intrapsychic matters, and this focus can be generated by the patient as well as the therapist. One of my patients told me, in all seriousness, "I think I have a problem with self-esteem; I feel jealous that my girlfriend is seeing someone else." Another patient, who had not worked much in the past five years, directed his therapy initially by talking about his depression, anxiety, and loneliness. At the end of the first session, I suggested that he find some kind of steady, meaningful work first and then assess his need for therapy.

Still another of my clients took a different tack. "I guess I should warn you, Dr. McCullough, that I didn't treat my last therapist very well," said Beverly. Since she seemed quiet and well-mannered, I was somewhat taken aback. "What do you mean, you didn't treat your last therapist well?" I inquired carefully.

"Actually," she confessed, "it wasn't just my last therapist; I've been pretty terrible to several of them."

With growing unease, I asked her again what she meant by that.

"Well, at some point in therapy I suddenly get furious. I feel like the therapist is telling me that my misery is all my fault; that if I just changed my thinking and my way of acting, I'd be cured. None of them wanted to deal with the real problem in my life—my husband. He says he loves me but he mistreats me. He buys me things, tells me he loves me, and then, out of the blue, he'll get angry over something and not speak to me for days. It's devastating. For years I thought it was me, and I'd try harder to please him. I used to think I was crazy, but I don't think so anymore, and when a therapist starts telling me I have to change, I just lose it."

It turned out that "losing it" meant that Beverly hurled an ashtray at her therapist. Literally, and more than once. She actually carried inexpensive little ashtrays in her purse in case any therapist tried to blame her for her pain.

Hastily, but truthfully, I reassured her that I felt that lashing out at her therapists was a sign of emotional health: She had been able to hold on to her reality in the face of everyone's (including the helping profession's) telling her that she was the problem. In my opinion, her ashtray-throwing was a case of self-defense in its most profound form. Too often, therapists treat the emotional reaction as if it were the pathology. Of course, I hoped that Beverly and I would be able, in future sessions, to explore alternatives to dangerous physical behavior.

Psychotherapy, more than recovery, sends mixed messages when you're suffering and want help. On the one hand, the professionals tell you they can cure you, and on the other hand, they maintain that you have to do it yourself. And therapy can be as overprotective as recovery. I cringe as I remember my early years as a therapist, just beginning to work with people who suffered from anxiety. Wanting to be the perfect therapist, not to mention wanting to feel successful at curing people, I would tell my patients to call me day or night if they were having a panic attack. What I did not understand was that, in making this offer, I was implying that I didn't trust them to handle the situation on their own. I created, or at least promoted, a dependent relationship, the seed and flower of victimhood.

MAYBE IT'S NOBODY'S FAULT

"It's all their fault" and "It's all my fault" represent extreme positions that bear little resemblance to lived reality. Our societal dilemmas demonstrate that it is extremely difficult to separate victim from victimizer. And when the victim and the victimizer are presumed to be the same person, the issue becomes even stickier. A false dichotomy arises from the victim/victimizer model: "If I don't blame these other people, then I have to blame myself."

"I've lost my job after thirty years and I'm very depressed," a man once told psychologist Bernie Zilbergeld.

"I understand that you're depressed, but I'm puzzled as to why you're wanting therapy. After all, your depression seems appropriate; it's a depressing situation," Zilbergeld replied.

While some might consider Zilbergeld's response to his prospective patient unsympathetic, I believe it is a necessary dose of honesty, and one that more therapists ought to employ. Americans, a "feel-good" culture, exhibit a profound distaste for our natural reactions to life's unpleasant episodes. When something bad happens, we are not only upset with the situation, we consider our instinctive painful reaction to be an abnormal, perhaps even a diseased condition. Then we feel sad about our sadness or anxious about our anxiety. Feeling sad about sadness often leads to misery, just as feeling anxious about anxiety leads to panic. The downward spiral continues.

"Mental health" may be the most abstract and confusing concept of all. "Am I normal, Doc?" is a question therapists often hear, in some form or another, from patients. But the label *normal* is even harder to affix than *dysfunctional*. Psychologist Sheldon Korchen offers five definitions: Normal is (1) not being sick or disturbed, (2) a desirable or ideal state, (3) a statistical average, (4) relative to one's culture, (5) the ability to adjust. You can waste a lot of time trying to figure out which of these definitions fit you, and what they actually mean. Does inability to adjust to an intolerable situation mean you're abnormal, and if so, is that bad? If you're only average, is that good?

"The normal," wrote W. Somerset Maugham, "is what you find but rarely. The normal is an ideal. It is a picture that one fabricates of the average characteristics of men, and to find them all in a single man is hardly to be expected." This, however, does not stop our postmodern society from determining that if you are unhappy, off the statistical bell curve of "average," a cultural misfit, or having difficulty adjusting to your current environment, you are abnormal. And that, if you are abnormal, you need treatment in order to blend in better.

To move beyond blame-laying, or pathologizing our symptoms of unhappiness, we must learn to stop finding the *reason* for our pain and focus instead on facing it head on. Here are a few suggestions.

1. Accept that bad things will occur in your life. Convinced that life is, or ought to be, fair and just, we deny evidence to the contrary. We hide this evidence—our emotional distress—from ourselves and from others. If life is arbitrary, how can we get a handle on it? We are horrified by the idea that fate can sometimes be cruel.

Alas, the fact is that bad things do happen, even to good people. ("Shit," as the bumper sticker proclaims, "happens.") Children develop fatal diseases. Earthquakes destroy homes, lives, and national budgets. And business "downsizing" throws talented, industrious people out of work. Efforts to eradicate the pain caused by these events represent a vigorous commitment to denial.

If we operated under the cultural assumption that life is tragic, victimhood would die. Who could complain of being victimized if that were the norm? The fact is, though, that life is neither tragic nor utopian. Life is a polarity; good comes from evil and evil from good. Positive and negative are the dance of life, a dance inherent in nature from atoms to Adams. Christianity, among other cultural mythmakers, attacks evil as though it were "Evil," but bad stuff is simply part of the nature of the world. If God creates the whole world, then it's not evil that we eat one another—it's natural. Trying to eradicate what we view as evil is a futile attempt to destroy nature. If the lion lay down with the lamb, it would starve to death.

To be in the world is to be in polarity, engaged in constant dilemmas. Victimhood arises from the denial of the necessary reality of bad stuff. Are there any good guys without bad guys to make them good? It's okay to say "ouch," but crying about it on national TV is whining about the truth of nature. *Owning* pain is the acceptance of the truth. Therapy, recovery, and the self-help business, however, support the cultural myth that pain must be attacked and bad stuff eradicated.

2. Admit to yourself that you don't control everything that happens to you. Because we believe we ought to be "in control," we feel guilty and ashamed when something negative slips past our guard. We have internalized that ominous dictum from the seventies, with which even cancer patients have been admonished: "You create your own reality." If reality serves up misfortune—and if we can't even control our *reactions* to this sad reality—we decide we must be dysfunctional and therefore in need of fixing.

Our lives ought to be happy; look at the Cleavers and the Huxtables—*they* have it together. Everything always turns out all right for them. Never mind that these are fictional characters.

Whether we feel victimized by biology, parents, or even our own selves, the feeling is underwritten by the American myth that life is, or can be, whatever we want it to be. We think our society (unlike the barbaric cultures in other parts of the world) is capable of winning wars on drugs, poverty, crime, disease, and boredom. So when winning eludes us, we think something is terribly wrong. Suffering then becomes embarrassing and inexcusable.

3. Recognize that pain and suffering can be a natural, evolutionary stage. The fact is that pain, once it's accepted, propels us into movement. Notice that I did not say, "Pain is a growth experience" or "Pain helps us change." I'm not convinced that most of us would seek change and growth if pain and suffering were the price. We are more likely to seek the security of changelessness.

Pain does, however, play a natural role in the ever-moving universe. If you assign it some "purpose," you overintellectualize it and remove it from its place in the flow of life.

Rosemary cried nearly every day for eight months following her husband's leaving their twenty-four-year marriage. Her emptiness could only be filled with her pain. She took antidepressants, forced herself to socialize, and kept turning questions over and over in her mind: "Why did he leave me?" "What did I do wrong?" "How could this have happened?" "What sense does this make?"

In our work together, Rosemary began to see that those questions didn't need to be answered in order for her to accept the simple reality of the situation and rejoin life. She had become stuck in her distress through fear of the change itself. Losing a relationship is epidermal, but the pain of insecurity goes to the bone. Rosemary's recovery was, to some degree, a consequence of her realization and acceptance of the truth about the world: It's not evil, but it is unpredictable and perpetually changing.

Declaring that pain is the price we pay for growing into a higher state of maturity and wisdom is very different from accepting the fact that life moves on with or without us. Whether the consequences of our pain are good or bad is, in a sense, irrelevant. What is relevant, in the movement through suffering, is the degree to which we accept both the pain of the loss and the pain of insecurity.

"Pain is pain—a simple painful fact," declares Michael Adam in *Wandering in Eden*. "Suffering, however, is only and always the refusal of pain, the claim that life should not be painful; it is the rejection of a fact, the denial of life and of the nature of things."

4. Allow others to see you suffering. Being in pain interferes with our self-marketing. Every day, millions of Americans gear up, make up, suit up, and cheer up for the marketing of the self. Nearly every move we make is calculated to sell ourselves in a competitive social or business marketplace. For a growing number of us, the selling of the self has become a full-time job. From the moment we wake up until day's end we are occupied with endless self-evaluations geared to determining and increasing our attractiveness in the eyes of others. So many of my patients confess to being *embarrassed* by their emotional pain—a clear indication that their suffering is to some extent up to other people.

Who has not, from time to time, put on a mask to impress others? Trying to present an upbeat image (and "image is everything," as a popular television commercial proclaims), we deny the dark side of life—as we deny our own shadow side. The shadow is comprised of those parts of ourselves that we do not want to acknowledge or deal with. These traits can be ones that we believe others do not like, or powerful ones such as sexuality that frighten us.

Whether we call it the "shadow self" or the unconscious or

the repressed self, denying it does not wipe it out. In fact, refusing to acknowledge and integrate it makes it stronger and more independent. Feelings that we do not confront directly go underground and affect us in ways outside our awareness and therefore outside our control. Denying suffering, a form of denying the self, actually increases suffering.

Others encourage us to keep denying our pain, so that *they* will not have to look at it either. Etiquette advice columnist "Miss Manners" related the complaint of a woman who became paralyzed on the left side by a stroke: "I am finally home, after spending thirty-five days in intensive care and five months in the rehabilitation unit, and people tell me how lucky I am. Lucky to be alive, lucky to be able to have physical therapy at the rehab hospital, and lucky my stroke was not worse than it was."

Rosemary, the abandoned wife mentioned earlier, felt even worse when her family, friends, and work associates heaped words of "wisdom" on her: "You'll see, you'll meet somebody who's really right for you." "You'll come out of this a better person." "One day you'll look back and see that this was all for the best." She began to feel guilty for feeling pain, and thereby turned it into prolonged suffering.

Until we understand that to a large extent our personal happiness is a function of the degree to which we accept *all* of who we are, we will continue to be at war with ourselves—a war that enlists the therapy business, with its arsenals bent on the eradication of unwanted feelings. Jimmy Swaggart had such hatred for his shadow side that he gave absolutely no conscious room to his sexual feelings, and they ultimately overtook him. He tried mightily to cast blame on others, and then tearfully blamed himself, but he lost his career anyway. Jimmy Carter, on the other hand, admitted that he "lusted in his mind" and avoided the taint of sexual scandal. People laughed at this admission—and inwardly identified with it. To be fully human, and free from the control of our hidden forces, we must have the courage to acknowledge all our potentialities—without blaming ourselves or others.

By de-pathologizing your emotional pain, recognizing it as a natural response to the inherent, fluctuating condition of an imperfect world, you can free yourself from having to spend the rest of your life reviewing, recalling, and retelling your woeful tale to therapists and support groups. By giving up the blame game, accepting responsibility without accepting guilt, you can own more of your own power—an important step toward health and freedom.

6

....

Step 2: Taking Back Your Own Feelings

It didn't take many sessions before my patient Lillian recognized that her anxiety was connected with feeling trapped by the expectations of others. She was the "good girl"—bright, polite, and ever so sweet. As she grew into her adult roles, she became the gentle mother, loving wife, and daughter who could always be counted on in any situation.

But, as Lillian put it, "I'm not that nice; if people knew what I was really thinking, they'd have me put away." Unbidden fantasies of escaping or just disappearing haunted her. Her anxiety, she realized, arose from what I called "gross acts of self-betrayal." She was trapped by her need for security, which she expressed by being a people-pleaser.

People-pleasers, who base their behavior on what they believe others want, are prime candidates for victimhood because they hand over to others the power to control their self-worth. Often they become resentful of these other people, then feel guilty for being resentful, then resentful again because they don't like feeling guilty. Living life from the outside in rather than from the inside out, they lose sight of their own values and their opportunities for freedom of expression. As someone once said, "The man who doesn't stand for something will fall for anything."

As a society and as individuals, we—even non–people pleasers —act in various ways that increase, or appear to increase, our sense of security in an uncertain world. If we believe that we all feel the same way, we can enjoy the solidarity of kinship. Rollo May points out, "The real threat is not to be accepted, to be thrown out of the group, to be left solitary and alone."

We want to feel that our pain is shared, and that it follows a well-defined pattern of thoughts, feelings, and behaviors, covering ground that others before us have trod. The great popularity of books such as Elisabeth Kübler-Ross's *On Death and Dying* and Gail Sheehy's *Passages* is in part due to their presenting objective descriptions that define certain stages of feelings and behavior. These descriptions imply that the feelings and behavior are universal, inherently true for all of us. We relax when we see such certainty, thinking, Ah yes, that's what we go through.

Seeking solidarity, we encourage others to believe that we all suffer the same: "Listen, George, I went through the same thing when Laura left me. You're going to feel really sad for about a year. Then you'll meet someone, feel tentative and afraid to get involved, and then slowly learn to trust. Here are the names of some books that will explain what's happening to you and your reaction to it. Good luck."

George has received not simply a caring ear, but also the equivalent of a pharmacy printout identifying side effects, allergic reactions, and dosage. We think that what worked for us will work for everyone else, even though we suspect that some of our personal values may not actually be shared by others.

A couple of years ago I conducted a survey of eighty-seven adults regarding their values. I was surprised when seventy-six of the eighty-seven said that they strongly or moderately agreed with the statement "I have a strong sense of my personal values." I was even more surprised when only nine said that they moderately or strongly agreed with the statement "Most of the people in the United States have the same set of values as I do." This certainly indicates how disconnected we are from one another.

We join support groups to treat our loneliness in this alienating society, or as philosophy professor Peter Koestenbaum puts it, "to share aloneness." While we sigh with relief at finding the company of fellow sufferers, we forget that huddling is not, in itself, community. A gathering of people who share fear and pain is not a network of life-enhancing interaction. But "suffering the same" at least provides a temporary feeling of belonging.

Validation Through Conformity

Our society honors individuality and at the same time works to eliminate it. Although we appreciate, applaud, and encourage the creative self, we also try to explain, define, and control it. From childhood on, conformity accumulates more rewards than individual quirkiness. Standardized tests—psychological, developmental, intellectual—examine how well we "fit in" and penalize us with low scores if we don't.

Daily, Americans are encouraged to seek validation by conforming. Advertising repeatedly tells us all how to eat, dress, talk, and consume. It does more than inform us that we will be happy if we buy this or that; it promotes the idea of sameness. Happy people look like this, happy people act like this, happy people use this product. The implication is that if you're slim, you work out, or you own a cellular phone, you're on the road to love and success. By the same token, if you don't resemble the images portrayed on the TV screen or in the magazine ads, your contentment rests on shaky ground indeed.

Even the most casual conversations are based on assumptions of predictability: "Of course you're a procrastinator—your parents were always late for everything."

Speaking in the second person has become an ingrained American habit: "Well, when you grow up in a poor family and dream of winning this tournament, and then you do win, you feel on top of the world; you want to go to Disneyland." This is not as trivial an issue as it may seem at first glance.

A patient said to me, "You know, you just get real frustrated when he treats you like that." "And I don't even know him," I responded. Beyond my personal feelings of irritation when people use the second person to include me in their purely personal feelings, I believe it represents a desperate need on the speaker's part to feel just like everyone else, to be accepted, to belong— and, by extension, to control the immediate environment.

Moreover, in addition to lumping listeners into categories in which they may very well not belong, such "I-removing" generalizations also produce a negative, limiting effect on the speaker. When I say, "Have a nice day," I experience myself very differently than when I say, "I hope you have a nice day." Here are some other examples:

I like what you're doing *vs.* That's a nice job
I'm unhappy that I lost *vs.* You feel bad when you lose
I care a lot about this *vs.* This is important
I'd like to rip her nose off *vs.* You feel like you'd like to rip her nose off

Owning one's own feelings is the essence of self-esteem and a protection against control by others. And in order to become nobody's victim, owning our experience must be non-negotiable.

(The astute reader will have noticed that book writers, including this one, often generalize in the first person plural by saying "We do such-and-such." I maintain that this is different from the above examples in that we *intend* to generalize. *We* are making a statement about society in general, not trying to avoid accountability for our individual feelings. Or so we believe.)

Self-help books, recovery, and therapy perpetuate this doctrine of sameness, offering formulas and generalizations that purport to identify and explain universal traits and experiences. Self-help books in particular are fond of presenting checklists to help you determine how much you are suffering. If you read enough of these checklists, you can begin to doubt yourself, as my friend Sidney's story illustrates:

> "I bought John Bradshaw's book *Homecoming* because I
> figured it was time to get in touch with my 'inner child,'
> or at least to find out what an inner child is. In the first

chapter, I found a 'Wounded Child Questionnaire' that was supposed to 'give you an overall view of the extent to which your inner child is wounded.' It contained sixty yes-no items, like 'In the deepest places of my secret self, I feel there is something wrong with me,' and 'I'm driven to be a superachiever.' At the end of the questionnaire was the statement 'If you answered yes to ten or more of these questions, you need to do some serious work. This book is for you.'

"Ten out of sixty—an indication that you need this book? Sounded like a marketing ploy to me. But as it happened, I answered yes to only eight items, and was ambivalent about some of those. At first I was relieved. Then I started to worry: Am I really in denial? Only eight out of sixty? Maybe I really *was* wounded but didn't know it, or wouldn't admit it even to myself. Although I hadn't felt the book had any relevance to my life, I couldn't be sure."

"Denial" is that no-win state inhabited by those who don't acknowledge feeling as bad as they are "supposed" to. Therapists, recovery associates, and friends will tell you that you just haven't gotten in touch with those feelings *yet*, "but you will—everyone goes through this process." If you exhibit the prescribed reactions, you are admitted into the victim club; if you don't, there may be something retarded about you and membership is provisional. If all that is required to gain the acceptance of a given group is admitting that you may feel as they do, why *not*?

If you do not agree that certain predictable responses are inevitable, you remain outside the club. "Universal" sufferings are connected to "universal" reactions. "We suffer the same" is the concept upon which the victim business rests. You're expected to suffer in just this way, so you'd better do so if you want to belong.

I love it when I go to the hardware store and find that the showerhead attachment comes in one size only. Standardization is wonderful when it comes to equipment. But I like my people in multiple sizes and varieties.

INTEGRITY AND EMOTIONAL WELL-BEING

The subjects of integrity, sincerity, and virtue are seldom discussed in social institutions, such as schools, workplaces, and even churches, much less in therapy and recovery groups. Yet these questions lie at the heart of human experience.

Much emotional pain results from the discrepancy between inner experience and outward expression. In a society that requires us to sell ourselves for profit or survival, we are all masters at disguising our genuine selves. We present a facade of cheery confidence when we feel distracted and sad; we hide our anger and sometimes even our love. As a result, we separate ourselves from ourselves as well as from one another. We feel somewhat ashamed of our phoniness, because we value integrity and honesty, yet we feel that these sterling qualities have to be compromised in a competitive world. Consequently, we become confused and unhappy.

Some years ago I conducted a simple experiment that reinforced what I had been observing on a casual, informal basis: I asked each subject to walk over to another person across the room, shake hands, and say hello. The other person then told a blatantly racist joke. The subjects had been instructed ahead of time to laugh and say how funny the joke was. A few minutes later, I asked the subjects to repeat the exercise, only this time to respond in tune with their honest feelings, which in the case of all these particular subjects were along the lines of "I don't think that's funny" or "I don't like those kinds of jokes."

For each of the twenty subjects, body language after the two encounters differed remarkably. Without exception, after the people-pleasing encounters, the subjects showed one or more of the following: head hanging down, somber or sad expression, head shaking back and forth, quickened pace. After the exercise in which they expressed their true feelings, their heads were up, their eyes alert, their expression confident, and their pace slower. They clearly did not feel sad or guilty. Even though they disagreed openly with their experiment partners, they felt the power of integrity: being in tune with their own truth.

Self-esteem is a hot issue today, and is sometimes misunderstood. When controversy about incorporating it into a school curriculum arises, someone is sure to point out that praising children for every little thing they do is not conducive to learning or to building a healthy society. They are right. Self-esteem does not depend on praise or even attention from others so much as on a sense of personal integrity. People feel self-esteem when they are true to themselves, and from this place of personal truth are able to give to themselves and others. If our everyday encounters with one another were more genuine and less dependent on the marketplace, we wouldn't need to hire professionals to give us honest feedback.

Socrates defined the "good life" as happiness which in turn comes from "virtue," with virtue itself a natural consequence of knowledge. He meant not just psychological knowledge, such as becoming aware of your guilt for rejecting your child, but a more fundamental kind, which is linked closely to integrity. Virtue is the degree of integrity with which you apply knowledge. As John Adams put it, "All sober inquirers after truth, ancient and modern, pagan and Christian, have declared that the happiness of man, as well as his dignity, consists in virtue."

Integrity and virtue mean being consistently true to your personal values—even small ones. Wallace Carr defined integrity as "using a butter knife when nobody else is around." Being true to your values means that you need to be clear on what those values are. Again, therapy and recovery drop the ball by not concerning themselves with questions of personal integrity and values. Recovery programs, in fact, present you with twelve steps that amount to twelve values: Value these and you will recover. Success is defined by how well you conform to the program values rather than how well you develop independence and live your personal truth. Therapists likewise project their own values onto you, rather than encouraging you to spend time identifying your own values, examining the relationship between certain values and emotional suffering, and adjusting or changing your values. As a result, much is lost in the healing effort.

The particular content of an act of integrity is less important than the selection of it. Re-identification of values, so that they are actively chosen rather than unconsciously or passively accepted, ought to be a central mission of therapy/recovery. There is something very natural in a healing process that involves issues of value. Such issues contain properties that specifically decrease feelings of victimhood:

Awareness→knowledge→virtue (integrity, sincerity, honesty)→responsible victimhood→the good life

ASSERTING YOUR SELF

Moving beyond victimhood toward freedom requires a healthy sense of self. You don't need to be perfect or totally free from hang-ups, but you do need some idea of your strong points and limitations, and particularly your uniqueness. Since any forced sharing that distorts or represses your individual differences is harmful to your sense of self, perhaps new types of questionnaires would be useful, in order to counterbalance the ones that focus on victimhood.

For example, you might try answering yes or no to statements like these:

- Although I don't mind hearing friendly advice from others, I don't feel I have to follow all of it.
- I believe that even when my experiences seem similar to others', there are some differences also.
- When others tell me about their own experiences, I know which aspects apply to my own and which don't.

- I believe that, although I'm not necessarily better than anyone else, I am unique and deserve to be treated as such.
- I usually feel free to tell friends when I have experiences or feelings that are different from theirs.
- I don't always do what others expect of me.
- I trust my own ways of dealing with problems.
- I have a pretty good idea of what my basic needs are.
- When I respond to questionnaires, I don't make, or agree to, artificial numerical distinctions such as "If I answered no to three of these, I need to do so-and-so."

When George was listening to his friend's predictions as to the quality and length of his suffering, he could have been saying to himself, "This is clearly my friend's experience and maybe I will experience something similar, but my reaction may be quite different."

Ironically, even though a central aim of therapy and recovery is to unchain us from old, destructive self-concepts assigned to us by others (such as our parents), what they do is assign new concepts to us. They continually invite, sometimes even subtly coerce, us into being just like everyone else. If we are not aware of this process, our lives become big self-fulfilling prophecies:

"You know, Lucinda, it's been three months since Alan left me. I know I should be in touch with my anger by now. All my friends keep asking me if I'm angry yet. My therapist, of course, thinks I'm really stuck and resistant. I think I'll get them all together and throw a fit just to get them off my back. I *am* angry, I guess—at least I'm angry at all those people who keep accusing me of hiding from my anger."

When therapists, recovery people, and friends tell you that you are supposed to suffer, you form an image of a sufferer and carry it inside. You then become vulnerable to any messages supporting this image that come flying your way. With each reinforcement, you internalize the sufferer and make it a more permanent part of who you are.

Although, as I pointed out earlier, feeling bad may be a natural and normal reaction to your current circumstances, it is also true that you can often choose the way in which you respond to various life circumstances and can even modify your feelings. The reason you don't choose more often may be that you don't realize you can. The societal message that you are supposed to feel and behave in a certain way is a very strong one. You need to ask yourself some penetrating questions:

• Do I want to change these feelings? Would my life be better if I felt different, or would it seem too unfamiliar? What benefits do I get from feeling bad? Care and attention? Relief from responsibility? Guilt-tripping someone? Sense of solidarity with other sufferers? Something to replace emptiness?

• Can I imagine myself feeling and behaving differently? Some people don't react the way I do; what do they do instead?

• What's keeping me from changing? This question demands honest and serious thought. The answers may involve anything from physical limitations to fear of other people's disapproval or disinterest.

• If I decide to stop feeling and behaving in this way, and begin feeling and behaving in a different way, how would I get started?

You can also assert the power of your individuality and choose a different perspective. In John Irving's *The Hotel New Hampshire*, Junior Jones says to Franny, who has just been raped by four men, "You know what? When someone touches you and you don't *want* to be touched, that's not really *being* touched—you got to believe me. It's not *you* they touch when they touch you that way; they don't really *get* you, you understand. You've still got *you* inside you. Nobody's touched you—not really. You're a really good girl, you believe me? You've still got *you* inside you, you believe that?"

Feelings and behavior do not always appear in that order, cause leading to effect. Behavior can change feelings. If you act as though you're feeling positive, you may notice that these feelings are coming true.

Change usually isn't easy, and it can take time. But exercising choice can begin to make it happen.

NEITHER A BUYER NOR A SELLER BE

Part of owning our own feelings is recognizing that if we're not buying, others can't sell us on what *they* think we should feel. Monica stopped by to say hello to her friend Sam as he and I were having breakfast at an outdoor café. While the two chatted, my pancakes arrived. Not wanting them to get cold in the cool outdoors, I poured syrup on them. Monica remarked, "That sure is a lot of syrup you put on your pancakes."

Reinforcing the security-giving assumption that "we're all the same," she was attempting to sell me the notion that there is a prescribed amount of syrup one should use, one that I had violated. I could have responded, "I always use too much syrup; it's a weakness," thus buying what she was selling and assuming ownership of what was actually her issue. Or I could have said, "I have excellent motor skills and have put precisely the amount of syrup I wish on my pancakes; what's your problem?" I would have then been, rather nastily, hurling ownership back at her.

What I actually did was respond mildly, "Too much, you think?" She looked a bit uncomfortable and finally said, "I didn't mean to be critical." I had gently handed back to the owner what she was trying to sell to me.

Sellers use terminology that invites us to buy into their perceptions:

- Why don't you ever show up on time?
- What's the point of doing that?
- That's a strange attitude.
- Why do you have to be so angry?

If they owned their own feelings, they would say, instead:

- I hate it when you're late.
- It doesn't seem necessary to me to . . .
- I have a hard time understanding your attitude.
- I feel really uncomfortable with your anger.

Psychological buying and selling takes place all the time in human interactions. Being a seller is more comfortable than being a buyer. Disowning our feelings takes the heat off us and puts the responsibility on the "buyers." They are the ones who have to explain, and we don't have to risk talking about our own sensitivities. The messages we send them also imply that we speak for the universe. If others buy into them, we are rewarded with a sense of power.

Sellers deny the uniqueness of those they regard as potential buyers. Monica was doing more than questioning my judgment, motor skills, or violation of some universal law. She was asking me not to be an individual. Too bad she didn't stick around long enough to see me butter my toast!

Healthy and productive communication requires acknowledging our own issues and also acknowledging the uniqueness of others. When other people attempt to sell us an issue that doesn't fit us, it is a kindness to hand it back to them—reminding them that we're not all the same.

Taking responsibility for your own feelings is akin to taking charge of your own life. If you view your medical doctors as advisers rather than gods, and assume responsibility for the care of your own body, you are likely to be healthier than if you delegate the guardianship of your physical well-being. After all, you have insider knowledge that the "experts" don't possess. Similarly, you can view recovery programs, therapy, and self-help books as resources that you use for your own purposes. You can pick through their insights and recommendations to find what fits your needs, and then balance the knowledge they impart with other healing activities and a trust in your own experience of reality. As the Arabian proverb says, "Keep what is worth keeping, and with a breath of kindness blow the rest away."

You are unique. Celebrate that fact, and don't let anyone try to sell you on how you "ought" to feel or be or do. To be nobody's victim means, in part, that you control the syrup.

7

Step 3: Asking the Right Questions

There is a layer of human nature deeper than psychology. Neither the Oedipus complex nor the archetype, neither the inferiority complex nor the need for safety are the ultimate factors in a human existence. It is not enough to uncover childhood origins of present-day neurosis. Each final psychological cause or ultimate explanation is in turn a symptom, a metaphor, or a symbol for an even deeper, underlying philosophical condition; the symptom is a manifest expression of the less obvious, less picturesque but nevertheless generic malaise, challenge, and hope of what it means, to all of us, to be human.

Peter Koestenbaum

People sometimes feel like victims even when they can't immediately identify a victimizer. They sense that something is sad or wrong or missing in their lives, and they feel unable to cope with this predicament. So they turn to therapy, recovery groups, or self-help books in an attempt to "get fixed." The irresponsible victim looks for the victimizer—someone or something to blame and perhaps punish—while the responsible one seeks ways to regain the power he feels he has lost somewhere along the way.

But while therapy and its offshoots can provide some very narrow insights and induce some temporary or even permanent changes in behavior, they fail to supply the ultimate answers because they are asking the wrong questions. Both the questions asked and the questions omitted can reinforce your feelings about being victimized, reduce the effectiveness of help, and keep you in treatment too long.

Therapy, recovery, and self-help programs are asking the wrong questions because these are easier to answer than the deep social and philosophical questions that lie beneath all emotional suffering. These purveyors of help, and often the consumers who seek them out, prefer to deal with neat questions and neat answers.

A recent infomercial selling videos and books on improving relationships claims to give you the "tools to enter a healthy relationship" if you learn how to avoid the "five emotional time bombs." The program also claims that you can learn how to change from anger to love "in three minutes." The ultimate in neatness! As I viewed this infomercial, I had an image of the lover being armed not with flowers but with pliers, a set of socket wrenches, an egg timer, and wire cutters to defuse the time bombs.

If you start off with a false, limited, or distorted question, there is little hope of arriving at a satisfying answer. So to complete your escape from victimhood, you must begin to look carefully at the issues that drove you there in the first place. In recovery and often in therapy, too, misery is generally presumed to be a direct consequence of some abusive situation. Yet a deeper awareness reveals that it arises from a conflict between the reality of human existence and the desire to hide from that reality by assigning metaphorical causes. For example, when someone you love rejects you, your feelings of isolation are not *created* by the loss but *uncovered* as a truth of the human condition: As an individual in the world you *are* alone. And this can be a frightening revelation we resist.

But refusing to confront a universal truth cannot make it go away or become untrue. And there is enormous healing in allowing truth into our lives, no matter how frightening it seems initially. I frankly never understand when people say, for example, "I don't like existentialism, it's too negative." So? Perhaps some truth hurts, but hiding from truth is ultimately more painful. If you acknowledge aloneness, you can actually avoid isolation. As spiritual leader J. Krishnamurti put it:

> There is a vast difference between isolation and being completely alone, integral. Isolation is a state of mind in which relationship ceases, when in your daily life and activity you have actually built a wall around yourself, consciously or unconsciously, so as not to be hurt. . . . Aloneness implies a mind that does not depend on another psychologically, is not attached to any person; which does not mean that there is no love—love is not attachment. Aloneness implies a mind that is deeply, in-

wardly without any sense of fear and therefore without any sense of conflict.

Psychotherapy and the self-help industry concern themselves with "fixing" people. But what is it that they are fixing, anyway? Treatment is considered "successful" if, for example, a person can stop using drugs. The question of whether he has successfully confronted fundamental human concerns is not even asked. But if the drug abuse is the symptom of a deep sense of meaninglessness and emptiness, then what sort of "result" is it that is defined solely as an end to negative behavior?

As I have suggested, the "why" questions that analytical therapists love so much tend to focus on personal pathology and/or early family experiences. The assumptions are (1) that the "why" questions must be answered, even if this means extending the therapy while probing more and more deeply, and (2) that if these questions are answered, suffering will end. Recovery contains built-in assumptions about "why" and goes right for the fixing.

But whether the therapeutic question is "Why?" or "How can this be fixed?," there are three significant dimensions of life that therapy and recovery consider off limits:

- Social and political systems
- Personal integrity issues
- Ultimate philosophical issues

By roping off their territory, these purveyors of treatment ensure their failure to treat the real, whole person. Can we really understand the pygmy tribesman by placing him in a New York City hospital to observe his behavior, or treat the Pope's depression without bringing up spiritual concerns? Hardly. And what makes the average therapy patient any different, except for a little height or a great white outfit?

THE DANGERS OF AVOIDING SOCIAL ISSUES

Therapy, recovery, and self-help books, as I have noted earlier in this book, look at their clients through a small peephole. For example, family therapists recognize that the suffering individual must be understood as she actually lives in a relationship or family. But although family therapy moves out from the narrow boundaries of intrapsychic conflict, chemical imbalance, and early-childhood development, even this form of treatment falls far short of addressing a person's total natural environment. Like other "healing" professionals, family therapists avoid dealing with questions of class, gender, poverty, unemployment, or hunger. They neglect fears of war and street crime. They ignore the emotional distress engendered by society's marketing messages. And they leave questions of public policy completely alone. The same is true for recovery groups.

Therapists and recovery gurus would justify their narrow focus by claiming that their professions are not designed as instruments of social change. Their job is to treat pain and save the wounded, not reform socioeconomic systems. People, they would say, need to take personal responsibility for their own feelings, rather than blaming society.

But since you don't exist apart from your social contexts, how can your wounds be treated outside them? If your workplace is coercive, stressful, and demeaning, "reframing" your thinking about it can go only so far in healing the pain and freeing you from victimhood. Taking responsibility for your feelings need not and should not exclude formulating some action to change the workplace.

When therapy or recovery focuses on just part of your context, it treats just part of you, and this is not only ineffective, it's dehumanizing and disempowering. It can even be damaging. Clinician and author Fred Newman points out that "the contradiction of traditional therapy . . . is that even when it works to help people to adapt to their society, if it's a reactionary, racist, sexist, homophobic, backward, alienate, classist society . . . if you develop a therapy which simply adapts people to that, then you do so only at the price of people being further removed from history, which means people being further mis-identified as who we are fundamentally as a species. To make people societally sane, using traditional therapy, you must make them historically crazy!"

Moreover, avoiding the larger social context lets society off the hook. Therapy and recovery, by suggesting that the client needs to change, implicitly accept—even support—the status quo. Focusing narrowly on the self not only promotes passivity, it drains energy from the kinds of social action that might address the real problems.

Jevon was fifty-three when he went to a therapist for the first time. He had had his ups and downs in life; his parents had divorced when he was fourteen, he had grown up poor, and, as a black man, he had not found success easy to come by. But he had worked hard and persevered, and for nearly thirty years had made a good living as a mechanic at a local dealership.

When he was suddenly laid off, with no warning and very little severance pay, he had two children in college as well as the financial responsibility of an elderly mother. After months of anxiety and depression, he, at his wife's insistence, made a therapy appointment. After listening to Jevon's story, the therapist recommended psychological testing, suggesting that he might have a personality disorder. Not once did the therapist express outrage over the way the company had summarily dismissed Jevon and failed to assist him in locating new employment. There was no discussion of practical actions Jevon might take against the company.

This kind of therapy is terrible not only for Jevon, but also for the society of which he is a part. Therapists like his are operating on the wrong patient. And Jevon's is far from an isolated case. I was shocked to learn that psychologists had advised the post office to improve its employment screening procedures to address the surge of violence against managers, rather than dealing with the abusive working conditions that stimulated employee anger.

When therapy and recovery treat your emotional pain in a way that distracts you from the fundamental facts of being-in-the-world, they conspire with your—and society's—own resistance to looking at the wholeness of reality. They legitimize the diversion and fill in for what is missing. And as long as the larger issues remain unresolved, emotional illness, restlessness, unhappiness, and victimhood persist.

ULTIMATE CONCERNS

Beyond immediate concerns such as the current romantic or family relationship, and even beyond the context of wider social systems, lie fundamental philosophical issues that affect us all: meaning, purpose, freedom, and death. At certain points in our lives, such as when we lose a job at the age of fifty, when a loved one dies, or when serious illness strikes us or someone close to us, we come face to face with these issues; they touch us deeply and often cause us to reevaluate the way we have been living our lives.

The rest of the time, however, these basic philosophical issues seem so abstract that we tend to ignore them, even though they go to the root of our emotional pain. Society rejects them as intangible—too spiritual or "new age" for our bottom-line mentality—and therapy and recovery likewise decline the opportunity to deal with them, offering instead various regimens of repair techniques. Faith in a mystery larger than ourselves, which does not lend itself to labeling, does not fit into the historical niche of the victim business.

My observations of patients have, for a long time, been telling me that there is a pervasive longing, a yearning, a cry for some deeper and more satisfying response to today's brands of misery than therapy and recovery are providing. This longing has begun to coalesce into demand: Investigations of the "soul" have spawned a number of popular books and articles. While most psychologists still cling to the insistence that their field is a science, others are reluctantly beginning to examine the implications of the fact that "psyche" means "soul," and are beginning to acknowledge that the understanding and treatment of human beings requires much more than a scientific view.

At one time, religion at least partially fulfilled the yearning for deeper exploration of ultimate, existential questions. But religion is bound up in dogmas, creeds, and belief systems that were built on the speculations of those who sought to control others. Like most therapy and recovery programs, religion offers only established sets of moral principles rather than providing an environment in which individuals come to search for meaning and purpose. Organized religion fails because, in exercising a kind of parental authority, it attempts to prescribe values rather than explore them.

Still, certain fundamental questions catch at our souls, among them:

- Who am I?
- What is love?
- What is the meaning or purpose of life? Of my life in particular?
- What is real?
- What represents my security?
- What do I truly believe in?
- How do I feel about death? About my own death in particular?

Such questions are thought to belong more properly to philosophy and to subjective experiences such as music and art than to psychology. This is one reason I find psychology inadequate, even embarrassing to me as a therapist. It can be cruel to pretend that cognitive restructuring or behavioral desensitization satisfies our need to fill our emptiness and our search for meaning, love, and peace. Reading philosophy, becoming absorbed in a good novel, or wandering through a museum can flood me with human understanding, whereas psychological research and analysis feel arid.

Newer, hipper forms of treatment can likewise be narrow and emotionally sterile. For example, just when you feel starved for love, nourishment, and deeper meaning in both your life and your therapy, along comes a new form known as "cybershrink," in which you interact with a computer terminal rather than a human therapist. One computer program, a sort of virtual psychotherapist, is called "Sigmund." This sort of technotherapy turns a deaf ear to (a) the importance of encounter, (b) the search for existential truths, (c) spiritual issues, and (d) social contexts. This has been a hidden shortcoming in the victim business all along; at least the concept of "me cybershrink, you cyberpatient" is honest.

RECOGNIZING THE REAL QUESTIONS

While "unscientific" issues such as reality and the soul, resonating with our deeper needs, are beginning to intrigue us more and more, it is rarely a conscious consideration of these issues that sends us into the maw of the victim machine. Yet they are always there beneath the superficial or "popular" symptoms from which we seek relief.

For example, anxiety is our number-one mental health problem, according to the National Institutes of Mental Health, and one that healing professionals treat every day. Within psychology's narrow band of concern, anxiety is seen as a collection of symptoms, including physiological ones such as profuse perspiration, racing heart, hyperventilation, dryness of the mouth, and weakness in the legs, as well as emotional symptoms of apprehension and confusion. The "causes" are presumed to include chemical imbalance, maladaptive learning, or a genetic predisposition perhaps complicated by traumatic emotional events. Extreme anxiety can turn into panic attacks and phobia.

Therapeutic understanding operates within the assumption that anxiety is an enemy to be attacked, a pain to be eliminated. Nearly all the self-help books on anxiety reflect this assumption: *Fighting Fear, Conquering Shyness, Overcoming Agoraphobia, The Anxiety Disease, Don't Panic,* and *Phobics and Other Panic Victims.* Anxiety support groups also focus on what each individual can do to get rid of the "disease."

If we simply ask, "How can we get rid of anxiety?" then the answer is confined to psychological and biological weapons against it. But if we ask, instead, "What is the meaning of anxiety?" or "What message does this anxiety have for me?" we break free of psychology's narrow band into richer understanding.

A patient, Santos, once reported to me an experience that he knew to be deep but didn't understand right away: "I was standing by the ocean, right near a steep cliff that led down to sharp rocks, when I suddenly realized that I could very easily jump or fall, and the only thing that was keeping me from doing either was my own free will. It was a terrifying thought." Santos had confronted the ultimate possibility of nonbeing and also the stark truth of personal freedom: Without railings to hold him back, notbeing had become a possible choice for him. As a result of this episode, and his confrontation with the extent of his personal freedom, Santos became extremely fearful of heights.

"Fear of heights" is not really fear of the high places themselves, but of falling and, more frighteningly, the freedom to choose to fall (or not to fall). This form of anxiety is what the Danish philosopher Kierkegaard meant by the term "dizziness of freedom."

Another way of putting it is that anxiety is not a disorder, it is a warning light on the dashboard: a signal that you are empty. It is a symptom of "looking inward and finding nothing," as Kierkegaard said. When you run away from anxiety or attempt to fight it, you turn it into a neurosis. Running from anxiety is running from freedom—our most defining quality. By turning attention away from meaning and toward "fixing," psychotherapy supplies the Nikes. But using therapy to mute the ontological message of anxiety, or turning your freedom over to a higher power, represents an assault on human value.

To "treat" anxiety by eradicating it is to deny the historical reality of anxiety and its relationship to the development of alienating social systems. Anxiety is a normal and natural response to the growing awareness of our own nothingness, or lack of values. We are anxious because of the incongruity between how we feel and how we must act to sell ourselves in a competitive social system. Abandoning our real self results in a "homeless," shaky feeling.

Anxiety might contain additional messages: It might be telling us that something of value is threatened, and that we are afraid of losing it. It also might be telling us that we are freer than we want to be—that we stand alone in choosing. (This issue will be explored further in chapter 10.)

All I have said about anxiety could also be said about addiction and a number of other problems that send people running for help. In fact, addiction is usually an effort to hide from anxiety and its messages. An addict is someone who definitely does not want to be reminded of nothingness, values conflicts, crises of meaning, or freedom to choose.

LIVING WITH UNCERTAINTY

Even worse than dealing with complicated answers, in contemporary American culture, is finding no answers at all. Answers are the goal, the end product that people zealously pursue. On the quiz show "Jeopardy" the answers are actually given before the questions. Questions that seem to have no answers seem like a joke without a punch line, sex without an orgasm, or boxing without a knockout. I've heard friends complain about a movie that didn't have a real ending or any real plot. These friends dislike art films that offer only portraits or observations of people's lives, films that simply say, "Look at this!"

Questions without definitive answers are generally avoided by therapy and recovery, which—reflecting contemporary social norms—focus on cause and effect. Confronting such issues as emptiness and ultimate aloneness is scary; it's safer to assign a concrete, immediate cause to our suffering. The larger issues, after all, do not lend themselves to "fixing."

Exploring questions about the nature of experience, its essence, can leave us with a feeling of uncertainty. Without quantitative measures and definitive answers, how can we solve our problems? Such concerns arise from a linear approach to life, an approach that ignores the value of being present in a dynamically evolving situation.

Both insight therapy and cognitive/behavioral therapy (including recovery programs, which, as we have seen, share many of its key assumptions) emphasize the objective and rational at the expense of the purely subjective. In a sense, then, they ignore the larger meaning of consciousness—the energy field that includes Emptiness, awareness, feelings, timelessness, the "is," the experience of the universal shining through the individual. (The term *emptiness,* with a small *e,* as discussed in earlier chapters, refers to a lack of meaning, purpose, and significance. This *Emptiness,* with a capital *E,* is used to describe what is sometimes referred to as "the void" or "nothingness.") Consciousness is like a beam of light or thread from the self to the world. Because it is subjective, consciousness resists being labeled or defined (as the above description illustrates!). Therefore, it is generally ignored by therapy and recovery.

Figuring out causes and precise remedies leaves out spontaneity and serendipity and denies the absurd and irrational. The world *should* "work," and if it doesn't, it's not fair and we're victims.

When we step back, we not only see more, we also touch the profound realities that emptiness reveals. Awareness is openness; awareness is "yes" to everything we see. Without labeling, we see the world as it presents itself. Labeling, judging, analyzing, evaluating all cut us off. "Judge not, that ye be not judged" can mean "I won't cut off from you if you won't cut off from me."

We are all part of the stream of life, the field of consciousness that flows around and through our experiences. Sometimes we experience that awareness poignantly, even unexpectedly, such as when we view a spectacular sunset or achieve a point of profound rapport with a friend. In these transcendental moments, we "lose ourselves" and paradoxically, at the same time, find ourselves.

When we do not experience the consciousness that underlies the self, we are trapped in the objective world, which needs to be figured out and dealt with. We have polarized the issue of unconsciousness versus perpetual reflection and have overlooked an *integrative* mode: awareness. Analysis and prescription interrupt the flow of consciousness. Moving beyond the objective to awareness requires stepping back and *not doing*.

Carlos Castaneda, in *Journey to Ixtlan*, is told by Don Juan, "*Not-doing* is very simple but very difficult. *Seeing*, of course, is the final accomplishment of a man of knowledge, and *seeing* is attained only when one has *stopped the world* through the technique of *not-doing*." Not-doing means seeing the world as it presents itself to you and not evaluating it, analyzing it, reflecting upon it, or acting on it. It is surrendering to simple consciousness, effortless awareness.

Krishnamurti tells us, "What is important is not to learn but to see and to listen. If you can see, you have nothing else to do, because in that seeing there is all discipline, all virtue, which is attention. And in that seeing there is all beauty, and with beauty there is love. Then when there is love you have nothing more to do." You don't need to wrestle, evaluate, analyze, or interpret— merely witness. Being fully present, just looking, can reveal more about your secure self than focusing on the "why" and "how" of your experience. Therefore, it can help in healing; as Deepak

Chopra says, "A person is beyond all suffering when he can think and act without disturbing the silent clarity of his mind."

Here's Krishnamurti again:

> Look, when you go out, when you walk in these streets, there are all kinds of noise, all kinds of shouting, vulgarity, brutality, this noise is pouring in. That is very destructive—the more sensitive you are the more destructive it becomes, it hurts your organism. You resist that hurt and therefore you build a wall. And when you build a wall you are isolating yourself. Therefore you are strengthening the isolation, by which you will get more and more hurt. Whereas if you are observing that noise, are attentive to that noise, then you will see that your organism is never hurt.

Awareness means setting up camp on a higher hill. The mountaintop has long represented what feels like a higher spiritual place. Seeing farther and more widely, you can experience pure consciousness and connection. There is healing power in awareness without analysis, and the content of that awareness gives heart to changes in behavior and thinking. It's not that we have to learn more; we simply need to *see* more.

Therapy and recovery tend to ignore the fact that sometimes the less one does the better. I often ask patients, during a session, to spend ten minutes peeling an orange. While most find the exercise boring, anxiety-producing, or irritatingly meaningless, some lose themselves and experience a sense of unity. Being quietly focused in this way encourages the practice of self-forgetting that expands awareness.

A rational person might ask, "Why pay a therapist to ask you to peel an orange? You could do that on your own." Therapists, I believe, can serve a valuable function by just being with the client, assisting in and encouraging the simple act of looking. As Lao Tsu put it, "One cannot see oneself in running water, only in still water; only the still can still the seekers of stillness." Sometimes the healer herself needs to step back and not do, together with the patient, and become a witness to the patient's unique process.

Marjorie began her session with me by declaring that her husband's behavior was unacceptable. She wanted to know what to do—how to change him, herself, or the situation. Only gradually did she become aware of the healing power of accepting the unacceptable. Acceptance is not to be confused with condoning or passivity; it simply means acknowledging the truth of the situation: "This is the way it is."

Once she had accepted this truth, Marjorie was able to move into a state of not-doing, of observing. From this quiet state she could observe herself in a larger context, taking in all the elements that did not fit the "abused wife" label. By grounding in what some refer to as the higher self, she could afford to be more aggressive in her refusal to be abused. The transcendent self gave her a home, a safe haven from which to act. Acceptance took the sting out of her painful situation, freeing her to "do" with a greater sense of power.

The appropriate role of a therapist or healer, it seems to me, is not to judge the patient or to focus on "getting better," but to assist the patient in balancing insight with action, left-brain (rational) with right-brain (intuitive), and personal with contextual. To do this, it is essential to help the patient build awareness and connect with a larger context through merely seeing: witnessing without evaluating. Unfortunately, most of modern culture and all specific therapeutic trainings militate against this approach. Unless the practitioners in the psychological healing professions can free themselves from the security of pathological explanations on one hand and the pressure for quick fixes on the other, they will remain locked into a self-perpetuating victim business.

Acceptance of uncertainty and insecurity, without trying to resolve everything, can be the beginning of the journey toward wholeness. Marjorie learned the advantages of not-doing partly through her "talk therapy" with me and partly through an extensive course in meditation. As is the case with many people who meditate, she eventually reported experiences of "oneness," a feeling of connection with the universe. Her desperateness subsided as she began to see—to feel—that her world was larger than her marital situation. Her sense of aloneness was replaced by that pure Emptiness that includes both good and evil, joy and suffering, truth and paradox. She acknowledged the reality of her marriage and of her aloneness, yet said she knew she was part of a universal consciousness.

The path toward clarity contains intrinsic satisfactions. Asking questions and progressing along this path are themselves healing—more healing than applying prescribed "techniques" to improve your marriage or cure your addiction to shopping. More satisfying than knowing about love, for example, is experiencing the very nature of love itself: its essence. Achieving this sort of awareness, however, requires personal commitment. Confronting the ultimate issues is confronting freedom—standing alone to choose in the face of not knowing the consequences.

I'll admit that doing this takes grit; accepting meaninglessness, ultimate freedom, and your inherent aloneness in the world at first may seem more painful than unemployment or a relationship gone bad. But confronting your pain on its literal, philosophical level will result in the deepest healing. By avoiding ultimate issues, you will doom yourself to, God forbid, more therapy and recovery time.

A continuous process fraught with uncertainty has its advantages over the pursuit of scientific cure. To claim "cure" is to deny the ongoing mystery of existence. When, in a mystery novel, the killer is revealed as the frustrated sister-in-law, the mystery is over and so is the novel. In real life, the mystery of the self is endless, which gives us hope for something eternal in our being.

Among those who are deeply engaged in the pursuit of life's ultimate mysteries, it's difficult to locate any victims.

LIFE OUTSIDE THE VICTIM CYCLE

....

8

Getting What You Need from Recovery and Therapy

People look to psychology for answers to problems of love and anxiety, hope and despair. What do they receive for answers? Either grossly oversimplified utopias, or gimmicks in the form of tests for everything, or technical books which "solve" the problem by throwing out the words. Love is thrown out and replaced by sex, anxiety is replaced by stress, hope becomes illusion and despair becomes depression. No wonder some serious and thoughtful students of our culture, like Gregory Bateson, believe that there is no science of psychology, and the whole discipline was a mistake to begin with.

Rollo May

What we need are more kindly friends and fewer professionals.

Jeffrey Moussaieff Masson

The "helpers" in the victim business are not all greedy, egotistical snake-oil salesmen with axes to grind and myths to perpetuate, to the detriment of those who seek their services. Most of them genuinely want to provide aid and comfort, and often they do. Just about all of us know people who, at a critical point in their lives, needed help desperately and found it in a therapist's office, a timely book, or the meeting room of a support group. Certainly, abuse and trauma need to be brought into the light and dealt with, not kept secret or buried beneath consciousness to avoid shame and guilt. Confronting personal issues—our situation and our current responses to it—is necessary for self-acceptance and to help us break old, self-destructive patterns.

In different ways, both therapy and recovery serve this purpose—up to a point, at least. However, as we have seen in previous chapters, they are limited in the same way in which the larger society is limited: asking the wrong questions, labeling, taking too narrow a view, not allowing for freedom and individuality.

Dealing with something is not the same as obsessing about it. Even if the therapist is highly ethical and competent, and the twelve-step group is full of supportive people, staying too long in psychotherapy or recovery (or both) can all too easily glue the "victim" label more tightly to your forehead. "I'm an ACOA, or an agoraphobic, or an incest survivor (never mind my other characteristics), and because of that I may not be able to survive on my own."

No matter how attractive the lures and perks of victimhood, the fact remains that *victims are not happy people.* Furthermore, therapy and recovery keep them focused on the negative. A particular evil done to you may have happened long ago, but if you keep talking about it, as the victim business urges you to do, it remains alive, perhaps even growing, in your mind. Thus you are doubly abused, once by the original abuser and again by yourself as you go over and over the abuse in your support group or your therapy sessions.

Abuse exists, and your need for support is legitimate. But if you are not to further victimize yourself by being stuck in treatment, at some point you need to get on with your life. Like welfare, treatment programs become detrimental, both to society and to the consumer, when they solidify into permanent lifestyles. Therapy and recovery serve as constant reminders that you are falling short of your potential.

There are two steps in outgrowing therapy and recovery, and thus freeing yourself from the victim trap:

1. Taking charge of your recovery or therapy program and making it work for you, rather than just being "in" it, and then determining the appropriate time to move on.
2. Finding nonrecovery, nontherapy sources for meeting your general, basic emotional needs, which therapeutic treatments can satisfy only temporarily and artificially at best.

This chapter deals with the first of these steps, chapter 9 with the second.

ASSESSING YOUR PROGRESS

I see [therapy] as a kind of building of doorways, opening conduits, and making channels, like a giant bypass operation, throwing in all kinds of new tubings so that things flow into each other. Memories, events, images, all become enlivened.

Michael Ventura

If you don't learn how to move through those doorways and conduits opened by therapy and recovery, you could make yourself a victim again by falling prey to their limited perspectives. You need to be in charge. Often my patients ask me, "How am I doing?" My response is, "I guess not very well, if you think that I know and you don't." I can, of course, share my observations, but they are colored by my own world of experience. I can know *about* their problems or *about* signs of their progress, but only the patient knows *directly*.

Even doctors, with their extensive backgrounds of study and experience, are not infallible. I wince when I hear someone say, "My doctor won't let me do such-and-such." It is never wise to passively turn oneself over to an "expert," since experts vary in their opinions, no theory fits all, and even a widely accepted assumption can be overturned by new evidence.

Yet people seldom take responsibility for defining for themselves the criteria for therapeutic success, and for assessing progress according to these criteria. They are aware of the feeling of crisis that drove them into therapy or recovery, and they may have been diagnosed with a specific problem or dysfunction, but they are unclear as to what recovery would look like. Then they tend to drift along without stopping to reassess their progress and their goals. They leave this assessment and reassessment up to the therapist or the group, and don't even insist on it from them. Such passivity is victim stuff.

Let's say that Julie comes to see me in order to resolve a troublesome relationship with her critical mother. I ask her what criteria, for her, would represent successful therapy. If the answer is, "Getting my mother to stop being critical," then I feel that resolution will be mostly a matter of luck. If, on the other hand, the answer is, "Finding ways to prevent Mother's criticisms from destroying me," I feel there is a real chance for success. However, it's not my perception but hers that counts. Her expectations will determine her attitudes and even her achievements in treatment.

Suppose Julie has, for six months, worked on raising her self-esteem and has become generally more assertive even though her mother has not changed. If Julie measures her success solely on the basis of whether her mother ceases being critical, then she may feel that therapy has failed. If, on the other hand, she sees her increased self-esteem and assertiveness as ways to insulate herself from her mother's barbs, her assessment might be positive.

While each patient or client must define for himself what constitutes therapeutic success, it's important to communicate this to the therapist or recovery group and obtain agreement. If the criteria are not agreed upon, hidden agendas may work at cross purposes. For example, I might be hammering away to get Julie to be more assertive, while the only thing Julie wants is some advice on how to get her mother to let up on her. The recovery group may be urging Arthur to confront his father's rage, while Arthur desperately desires support for moving out of the house. Lee may feel that he has reached his goal when he can stop at one drink during an evening, but his AA group may gasp in horror, declaring that only total abstinence signifies success.

Just as it's important to determine the criteria for success at the outset of treatment, it's also important to pause and reflect periodically, along the way, on the process and results to date. Your situation or goals may well have changed.

Here are some goal-setting and assessment guidelines that may help you use therapy and recovery to best advantage:

1. Make a list or write a paragraph or two about how you're feeling as you enter treatment.

2. In the first session, state your criteria for success and ask your group/therapist to state theirs. Are your goals congruent with those of the therapist or group? For example, do you feel that anything is possible, but the therapist insists on setting "realistic" goals? Or does she tell you you can do anything when you feel hardly capable of doing small things? Does the therapist or group ignore or disparage certain issues in your life, such as social or workplace pressures, that you feel have a bearing on your problem? What are the consequences of these gaps in assumptions? Remember, the limits to your potential for change at any given time are not defined by external criteria, but by your own assessment.

3. Spend some time at regular intervals—once a month or once every two months—evaluating where you are in relation to your criteria. Refer to the paragraph or list you wrote just before you started treatment.

4. Ask others—group members, friends, family—if they have observed any changes in you. Ask them to be specific.

5. Reexamine your criteria after a few months. Have they

changed? If so, write down your new criteria and discuss them with your group or therapist.

THE PROMISE AND REALITY OF TREATMENT

Assessment and reassessment criteria need to be based on realistic ideas of what can be expected from treatment programs and self-help prescriptions.

Often I am amazed at my patients' capacity for transformation—and sometimes I am amazed by their intransigence. After all, the lightbulb has to really want to change. While recovery programs, psychotherapy, and self-help regimens generally ignore individual differences in promising across-the-board salvation, discreditors of such treatments fail to appreciate human potential. Prescribing limits leaves out not only unpredictable human variations but also the mysterious and magical. Some research is now focusing on "quantum change." Health and Fitness News Service writer Madeline Drexler provides an example: "Driving home from an Easter worship service, a woman feels a 'tremendous sense of awe, peace and joy,' puts years of depression behind her, and never again has a drink or a cigarette." Quantum change is defined as a metamorphosis so profound that it involves new sets of personality traits, values, and/or attitudes.

Such dramatic shifts come suddenly—like AA cofounder Bill Wilson's transformation of spirit. Psychologists attribute them to flashes of clarity or a sudden realization of the incongruity between one's values and one's daily life. Although nobody is sure exactly what types of quantum change endure or why, the many case examples collected by those who study the phenomenon provide a fairly good reason to take magic seriously.

But while change—even significant change—is possible, you need to be clear-sighted about what catalyzes your personal growth:

• *Be aware of how the therapist's or the group's biases will affect your treatment.* For example, a great many therapists take the position that you can't change anyone else; you can only change your attitudes and responses to another's behavior. A patient told me that her previous therapist had advised that she try to communicate more clearly so that her husband would not get so angry with her. Others (and I am among them) think we tend to give up too early and too easily in confronting an abuser. We can do more than learning to live with him, improve our manipulation of him, or simply maneuver ourselves around him. Saying "Stop it" or "Don't talk to me like that!" at least recognizes the reality that the other person is the problem, and that it's not okay for the abuse to continue. If this does not change the abuser's behavior, it at least moves the partner out of the position of passive victim.

• *Be realistic about how healing progresses.* Many clients assume that "success" in therapy means unbroken progress upward toward freedom from symptoms. They become disheartened when uncomfortable situations or feelings recur after they thought they were free of them. But a bad day does not a setback make.

For example, I worked with Lawrence for several weeks on his public-speaking phobia. We arranged for some "safe" practice situations and also explored some of his underlying issues regarding fear of evaluation by others. After several successful speaking engagements, he experienced one in which he was extremely ill at ease. While he was able to deliver the speech, and people actually complimented him, he could not accept his discomfort. He came to me the next week quite distraught, feeling that he had lost all the ground he had gained. I reminded him that only his own attitude would make that true. The natural rhythm of life involves ups and downs, expansion and contraction. No one is perfectly happy or at peace for very long, no matter how many therapy sessions or twelve-step meetings they attend.

• *Don't assume that turning your life around requires turning your personality around.* Ellen, who sought my services because she was experiencing anxiety every day, agreed to consider that there might be a connection between her anxiety and her tendency to be a people-pleaser. However, she became even more anxious when she thought she would have to become a mean person in order to cure her anxiety. I told her that her sensitivity and thoughtfulness toward others was admirable, and I wished more people had these qualities. Ellen simply needed to balance her caring for others with self-care. She needed to integrate, not change—to become *more*, not *less*, of who she was.

Making the most of therapy and recovery requires that we recognize and integrate all parts of ourselves. Health, mental or physical, is a question of balance. It's only when we try to wipe out some quality within us that symptoms arise. As noted earlier, denying our shadows—those feelings or parts of ourselves that we wish weren't there—only drives them below awareness, where they have a chance to sabotage us. Integrity, an anti-victim trait, means acknowledging who we are in all our full context.

Your Right to True Therapeutic Encounter

As I've said throughout this book, each of us is a being-in-the-world, a consciousness-body-world continuum, or a "citizen of the field," as Deepak Chopra calls it. We are not separate from our context; we *are* our context, continuously influencing other elements in that context as they influence us. We are, at once, distinct individuals and inseparable parts of a larger whole. As waves, we flow into one another; the boundaries between you and me are artificial and thin. Quantum physics has determined that the nature of reality is dynamic relationship, not isolated units of matter. Nothing is really knowable in isolation. Viewing the entire field, on the other hand, is more likely to lead to healing, connecting, embracing, encounter, and description (as opposed to labeling).

If a therapist cannot encounter you in the largest possible context as a being-in-the-world, then you become an artificial construct—for example, the obsessive/compulsive who comes in at three P.M. on Thursdays. No matter how supportive, caring, and insightful the therapist is, if Angela is treated purely as a victim of her own inner conflict, she will have trouble outgrowing the therapy. Similarly, if the twelve-step program does not consider factors other than John's alcoholic wife, John will have trouble moving on as long as his spouse continues to drink.

In the therapeutic environment, two (or more) beings-in-the-world interact. One day, having seen three patients in a row, I thought how much my work required a process similar to what actors go through. You often hear actors talk about how, in order to play a certain role, they tried to dig deep within themselves to find the part of them that is like the character they are to play. My first patient that day was a thirty-two-year-old truck driver, the second a young housewife, and the third a sixteen-year-old high-school student. I have been or could have been any of them in some dark corner of my psyche. And if I can bring it forth, it gives the patient and me a place to meet.

Authentic therapeutic encounter is transcendent, engaging, and attending, and practicing it is an art. Encountering someone means that "both persons are changed," says psychologist Rollo May. He reminds us that "C. G. Jung has pointed out rightly that in effective therapy a change occurs in *both* the therapist and the patient; unless the therapist is open to change the patient will not be either." Still, many (if not most) therapists would rather play the all-knowing parent than risk the vulnerability of a real relationship, so they keep their professional distance.

Making the most of therapy and recovery requires you to acknowledge your entire context and insist that your therapist or recovery group does, too. Questions to ask, in assessing and reassessing the treatment process, might include:

1. What is the context of my life that makes me feel like a victim?
2. Do my therapist or fellow support group members ask me about, or seem interested in, my
   • Values?
   • Medical problems?

- Nutrition?
- Level of exercise?
- Work environment issues?
- Financial situation/concerns?
- Religious/spiritual beliefs?
- Social involvement?
- Political views?

3. Is my group or therapist open to change? Is a real encounter possible?

If the answer to the last two questions is "No," you may need to find a healthier form of treatment.

Ram Dass used to say that "therapy is as high as the therapist is." Assuming that he meant "high" as a level of consciousness, I agree with him. If your therapist is an analyzer or a fixer, then the therapy is not very high. I have known many therapists who are in conflict between their training and their personal level of awareness and understanding. They may feel spiritually in tune with Buddhist philosophy or existential issues, yet "do" therapy in ways that do not integrate those ultimate concerns. Their "professionalism" takes on a life of its own, overriding or hiding greater truths that they privately enjoy.

These therapists may not be doing the kind of work they would like to do because their patients, reflecting society's attitudes, are impatient and insurance does not respect the "higher" approach. When responding to the patient's need to be cured or fixed, even an enlightened therapist can fall back on treatments based on old, linear, cause-and-effect assumptions.

NOBODY'S VICTIM

I recognized this discrepancy in my own practice during the course of writing this book. A patient reported that his wife always discounted him when he told her how he felt about something. I impulsively responded, "What do you do that leads her to do this?" As I heard these words coming from my mouth, I groaned silently to myself, "I can't believe you're asking this question—blaming the verbal abuse on the victim." Much to my surprise, and embarrassment, and ultimate delight, the patient got angry and told me that therapy had always done this to him, sooner or later. A productive conversation ensued, and I did what no therapist as an authority figure likes to do: apologize. I explained that I was struggling to free myself from old habits that were a part of my training. My behavior had lagged, in that moment, behind my level of awareness.

Occasionally I see patients who are "high" themselves, and this makes it easier for me to explore wider and deeper issues with them. If patients don't raise or even hint at such issues, I admit I'm reluctant to do so myself. If Jerry just wants to get rid of depression and I start talking about the nature of consciousness, this could end up being the shortest-term therapy on record. Yet I believe that both patients and therapists would do well to risk more in exploring a wider band of awareness. Gradually, we can chip our way past the safety zone defined by the idea that treatment is exclusively an intrapsychic or intrafamily matter. Encouraging each other, we can start with an exploration of the patient's worldly context and move out from there into more spiritual matters.

Author and lecturer Thomas Moore declares that we need to "make the shift from psychotherapy as we know it today to care of the soul." He defines "soul" as a "quality or a dimension of experiencing life and ourself," something that "has to do with depth, value, relatedness, heart, and personal substance." To tend to the soul requires not-doing: "By doing less, more is accomplished," says the Taoist Lao-tzu.

Of course, if I am to be a not-doing kind of therapist, I have to prepare myself to respond to a potential patient's question: "What do you do?" or "What is your approach?" "Oh, I do a lot of not-doing in my practice" contains obvious marketing snags. Perhaps, since I believe that pointing to the power of nonbeing is a neglected process, and that ultimate issues are central to a person's escape from victimhood, I could call my work "applied philosophy."

What would an authentic encounter between an applied philosophy therapist and a patient look like? It might begin in a way similar to an encounter with a Zen master. If a patient reported, "Dr. McCullough, my wife just left me!" I might respond, "Have some tea" or "Let's paint" or "Listen to this Mozart."

This approach is not an avoidance or a disrespect of the patient's pain, but rather a way of reminding him of the broader context within which his pain is occurring. I believe that the greatest value of therapy is in revealing consciousness and freedom to the patient regardless of the presenting problem. The experience of consciousness—and the way out of victimhood—is a process of not-doing, acceptance, surrender, nonattachment, and letting go of the self.

Another powerful form of not-doing involves the healing properties of silence. Here I am not referring to the manipulative silence employed by a therapist who, by refusing to respond to a remark, forces the nervous patient to continue talking. I mean a silence jointly agreed to, one that could be suggested by either the therapist or the patient. "Let's just sit here for ten minutes and see what comes up for each of us during that period." This, incidentally, is a procedure that has been used to great positive effect in conflict resolution and group meetings. In addition to revealing hidden feelings and memories that bear on the problem, it widens the span of consciousness to include more context.

CALLING THE SHOTS

As a client of therapy and recovery, you have more options than simply putting up with an inadequate process, leaving treatment altogether, or finding another "healer" more in tune with you. You can take charge and change the direction of the therapy yourself. Therapists and even recovery gurus, many of whom are highly educated, usually have more to offer their clients than the clients ask of them, and may very well respond on different levels if encouraged to do so. As people, they have feelings and thoughts about areas of life that are typically omitted in the context of the usual therapeutic process.

A colleague reported to me that a patient had asked him if he had been "saved." As an atheist, the therapist had asked, "From what?" (Those atheists can be real smart-asses.) The therapist had then continued, "Whether I'm a Christian, Jew, or Hindu isn't important. These issues won't get in the way of your treatment."

I consider this an arrogant position. My colleague would probably have responded in a similar way if the patient had asked, "Do you have experience working with Hispanic American clients?"

"No, but your problems originate elsewhere; whether you are American Indian or Chinese American, you need to change your behavior, thoughts, or attitudes. Therapy has nothing to do with cultural kinds of things."

If your therapist responds in the way this colleague did, then you need to find another therapist. It's bad enough that affiliation and environmental issues do not occur to the therapist in regard to the patient who is sitting before him, but when you invite the therapist to address these issues and she declines, you have a sure indication that you will not be seen as a total being.

Every aspect of your experience as a being-in-the-world is relevant to therapy: your neighborhood community, family, work organization, ethnic community, gender identity group, political affiliation, economic status. Authentic therapy must be open to all aspects of a life. If you are an emotionally abused, Japanese American lesbian who is Catholic, what sense does it make to see a therapist who simply tells you you need to change your thinking? This doesn't mean that you have to find a therapist who mirrors your set of life circumstances, but the therapist must, first and last, want to witness you as a consciousness-body-mind-world continuum: a total person, not a fragment.

You need to find your own way of expressing this concern before starting work with a new therapist—for example, sending letters to several therapists asking them if they work this way. If you are already in therapy and feel that your therapist is closing off certain issues, you may need to bring this issue out on the table. You may be fortunate enough to find that your therapist is quite capable and helpful in discussing your experience of yourself in your various contexts, as well as existential or spiritual matters. Because of her training and society's usual expectations, she may have the uneasy feeling that she is not doing "proper therapy" if the discussion moves outside the parameters of intrapersonal and interpersonal conflict, but if she sees these issues are of equally great concern to you, she will be encouraged to continue with a holistic attitude. I recommend that you be very direct about this need and let her know rather than hoping she will figure it out.

Making the Final Break

Once you have experienced satisfying encounters and achieved the goals you have set for yourself in therapy or recovery, you have begun to outgrow the process, and it is time to consider moving on. This does not mean that, to be "nobody's victim," you should terminate treatment abruptly or prematurely. To "outgrow," my dictionary tells me, is "to lose or discard in the course of maturation." Outgrowing is a natural movement from one stage of development to another. Your recovery group or therapy sessions will come to seem superfluous, a figurative security blanket that you will relinquish naturally, as children do actual ones, when it is replaced by maturing interests.

For many years I have told my patients that the purpose of therapy is to get out of therapy. But I do realize that terminating is often more easily said than done. Dependency may still exist long after the presenting problem(s) have been successfully resolved. A patient faces many sources of resistance that impede or stymie the decision to leave, even when the timing is right.

These powerful forces include at least one, usually more, of the following:

1. Attachment to Emotional Perks

As psychologist Allan Bloom comments, "Who wants to leave [therapy]? There's no other situation like it on earth: For one to five hours a week, this person pays complete attention to you, only you. You haven't had that since you were six months old. You don't get that from your wife, or your kids, or anybody. Why would you want to leave?"

Right, who cares if you stay in your therapy or recovery group for thirty years if it feels good to you? Couldn't we all use a supportive, nonjudgmental person to tell our troubles to? The answer, of course, is that staying in this comfortable womb keeps you from growing up and experiencing the full context of your life. Emotional dependence, a form of victimhood, puts you in a powerless position. If you are a dependent person, you are hobbled, prevented from acting on your own behalf, from discovering new things about yourself in the world.

Although psychotherapy and recovery both preach "taking responsibility for yourself," the nature of the therapeutic relationship itself, and the subtle and not-so-subtle messages in recovery, may breed emotional dependency. If the caregiver likes the role of comforting the insecure (perhaps because it gives her some security of her own), you can all too easily fall into, and become attached to, the role of the comforted insecure person.

My friend Melanie told me that she just wouldn't know what to do without her therapist. "She really understands me. She pushes me to act independently. We have such a good relation-

ship—she'll even let me call her anytime if I need to; she's great."
I didn't have much trouble detecting a double message there.

2. Reluctance to Upset Others

You may be afraid that your therapist or group will feel let
down or offended if you suggest termination. The therapist or
group may reinforce this fear. Your therapist's face may show a
flash of disappointment when you bring up the idea of termination; your recovery group may act hurt when you miss meetings,
and may convey the message that your addiction requires a life-
long commitment. But this is actually a sign of the progress you've
made; the more authentic the therapeutic encounter is, the more
your therapist or group is likely to miss you (and you to miss the
therapist or group).

3. Self-Doubt

Doubt, particularly self-doubt, has plagued mankind from
the day he became self-conscious. Philosopher René Descartes
went to the bone by doubting everything, including his own existence. And now quantum science has emulsified our very substance. That we are waves and space, and not real sets of
particles, confounds our search for the indubitable. Deepak
Chopra points out that we are 99.9999 percent empty space; does
anyone feel a draft?

With society, the media, and the "helping professions" labeling and defining virtually all our behaviors, everything we feel and
do is suspect. Every question a therapist asks is, among other
things, an invitation to question and create self-doubt in the patient. Consider this hypothetical therapy session:

THERAPIST: Tell me, Raymond, why is it that you feel so angry toward your boss?

RAYMOND: Well, he passed me over for promotion even though all my evaluations were excellent and I had seniority.

THERAPIST: Does your boss remind you of anyone else?

RAYMOND: Not really. Oh, he's about the same age as my grandfather, I guess.

THERAPIST: How do you feel about your grandfather?

Before the end of this session, Raymond has either discredited his feelings toward his boss about being passed over, or has begun to wonder if his feelings are "just" about the promotion and not a manifestation of some hidden resentment toward his grandfather.

Patients come to therapy, or a recovery group, with the assumption that the therapist/group knows more, maybe vastly more, than they do—and the therapist or recovery guru may be more than willing to think so, too. Together they create a strange dance in which the more self-doubt the client experiences, the more successful the therapy feels.

In a somewhat perverse way the therapist, perhaps mostly subconsciously, takes pride and satisfaction in coming up with one brilliant insight after another—insights that are cleverer than the patient's own. A colleague once told me how he became aware of feeling resentful when one of his patients came up with her own insight. "Luckily," he reported, "I was able to look at my response; I was about to discount my patient's awareness." But as you know by now, if your insight doesn't come from within, it can contribute to dependency.

If you are attached to therapy or recovery, you may become afraid of losing emotional footing should you venture out on your own. You may also be fearful of giving up the labels that at first seemed so comforting. Who am I, you may wonder, if I'm not an ACOA, an agoraphobic, a shy person, a "survivor"? Remaining in therapy and recovery, however, may keep you from finding out. And surely that's the greater danger.

4. Lethargy

When I begin to feel bored in sessions with a patient, I suspect it is time to plan termination. Of course, it takes more than feeling bored; I must also have an intolerance for being bored. If the patient remains dependent and therefore tolerant of a bored therapist, and the therapist is willing to suffer boredom—for his own dependency reasons—the sessions can continue even though the therapy has essentially ceased to exist.

Someone has to break the impasse, and if it isn't your therapist or group, it has to be you.

To evaluate whether it is time to consider leaving therapy and recovery, and to assess what stands in your way, ask yourself the following questions:

- Have I achieved the goals I set for myself? As I have resolved each issue, does my therapist or support group tend to bring up new ones, thus keeping me in treatment? Does the therapist/group refer to negative experiences as "setbacks"?

- Are my goals still congruent with those of my therapist or group?
- Do I have a sense of wheel-spinning? Am I bored? Does my therapist seem bored?
- Have I discussed termination with the group or therapist? What was their response?
- Am I prepared to abandon victimhood? Is it okay to stop punishing my abusers through my suffering?

Don't make the assumption that everything in your life needs to be addressed and resolved before you terminate. It's tempting to want to win the mental health equivalent of the Good Housekeeping Seal, but your life will always contain new challenges. The question is, Can you meet them without constant reliance on therapy and recovery?

Outgrowing treatment rests in large part on identifying what is possible and desirable at this point in time. Without this clarity, you can remain trapped in an endless search for something that "works."

9

Outgrowing "Help"

Loss of community isolates man, and the mounting pressure of vast institutions and organizations, far from shoring up his being, only intensifies the alienative process: by fragmenting him into the mechanical roles he is forced to play, none of them touching his innermost self but all of them separating man from this self, leaving him, so to speak, existentially missing in action.

Robert A. Nisbet

Regardless of how successful you may have been in getting your needs met in therapy and recovery, the world still awaits you. Unfortunately, the more effective you have been in therapy and recovery, the more resistant you may be to moving on. The better the therapy is, the more it is unlike the larger and emptier social environment. You probably went into treatment because you were unhappy in your world; your life situation may, in fact, have been "making you crazy." If you got some important needs met in therapy or recovery that you couldn't get met on the "outside," going back out is likely to be an unattractive idea. You may feel like a homeless person who has been served a Thanksgiving dinner and then sent back to the cold streets.

Even if you have found some relief from your pain in therapy and recovery, it is important to remember that absence of pain isn't enough to make a life. Drugs or therapeutic techniques can alleviate symptoms of meaninglessness, but the meaninglessness itself has not been successfully confronted. Since the victim business is based on the medical model, you're considered fine if you don't hurt. However, you may not be fine at all.

Conversely, a bit of disequilibrium does not indicate that you are not "fine"; the pursuit of meaning in life can be a difficult road at times. "Fine," to me, implies that you are dealing adequately with the process, not that you are living in constant triumph. You can be wrestling painfully with the meaning of your life and still be fine.

In the same way that you assert your needs in therapy and recovery, you must also do so in the "outside" world. Until you can find avenues to what you need socially, politically, and economically, you may find yourself moving around in a victim system, going from one recovery group to another, attaching to gurus, or becoming addicted to therapy or self-help literature.

You need more than fifty dollars and a new suit when you leave therapy or recovery. You need to create situations that provide you with authentic experiences of what the victim system supplies synthetically: love, belonging and connection, security, self-esteem, meaning, and understanding.

The central question of this chapter is "Is there life after therapy or recovery?" The answer is yes, if we as individuals and as a society can find ways to establish teams rather than gangs, community rather than cults, awareness of self and others rather than reliance on religious dogma.

EMBRACING YOUR INNER ADULT

Getting your needs met in authentic ways requires, in part, developing skills and attitudes that carry you to a higher level of maturity. Looking at the world as an adult—complete with adult abilities and responsibilities—rather than as a wounded child offers an entirely different type of experience. Generally, therapy and recovery focus on what is *absent*: caring from parents, support from spouses, a sense that life is meaningful. *Outgrowing* treatment means focusing on what *does* have meaning, what *does* provide support. It means developing character, not just fixing problems. And it means actively connecting with the larger context of life.

Researcher Mihaly Czikszentmihalyi studied more than a hundred thousand individuals from all walks of life, around the world, to determine what made people happy. He and his research team concluded that when people are so involved in an activity that nothing else seems to matter, when they manage to connect all their experience into a meaningful pattern, they feel in charge of life and feel that life makes sense. They enjoy themselves. This can happen despite adversity; in fact, struggling to overcome challenges can increase enjoyment.

"Contrary to what we usually believe," he reports, "moments like these, the best moments in our lives, are not the passive, receptive, relaxing times—although such experiences can also be enjoyable, if we have worked hard to attain them. The best moments usually occur when a person's body or mind is stretched to its limits in a voluntary effort to accomplish something difficult and worthwhile." Pleasure in itself does not bring happiness. What does, he concludes, is loss of self-consciousness: self-forgetting, a feeling of union with the environment.

Action and involvement are potent ways to relieve the symptoms of depression and emptiness. Nothing parts the dark drapery of victimhood better than forward movement—movement toward connection with the self and with others.

In moving on, you need to focus more on recovery *of* (your creativity, your support network, your joy) than recovery *from* (abuse, depression, family dysfunction). This requires you to ask yourself some pretty fundamental questions:

- What has meaning for me?
- What gives me joy?
- How do I define the good life?
- What kind of environment would contribute to my emotional well-being?
- How can I bring beauty into my life?
- How can I express my feelings without self-pity?
- What are my values, and how can I express them?
- If I'm no longer in therapy or recovery, to whom can I tell my story, and how shall I tell it? With whom can I be open and honest?
- What nobler purpose could my life serve?
- What will allow me to look back on my life without regret?

After his father's death, Harry told me his father had seemed like a ghost in Harry's life. Never critical or abusive, he had worked and provided for Harry, his two sisters, and his mother. "And he was very good at it, too," said Harry, on the verge of tears. "But I just don't have the slightest idea who he was. When he expressed affection toward his grandchildren, it really upset me. I would have loved to have had even a little of that."

Harry later added that he'd always envied his best friend, Brad, whose father was a simple man and who could not afford many of the things that Harry's father could. Yet Brad and his father played together, laughed together, and engaged in serious discussions with each other, and the father went to all Brad's activities. Who knows how he escaped the killing seductions of a competitive consumer society. Harry's father's life, by contrast, was a stunning success by society's standards—but he lacked what some would call A Life. His story is a chilling reminder that we must fight for emotional satisfaction, insisting—against the tide of social, political, and economic pressure—on a life with quality: the "good life," rich in both internal satisfaction and connection.

One facet of healing is connection with the self. One way this can be accomplished is by focusing on meaningful pursuits and expanding your cultural horizons. Roberta Jean Bryant, author of *Stop Improving Yourself and Start Living*, explains: "The arts are healing. Whether you're moving your body in dance, mime, or juggling; making music; creating or capturing visual images; working in wood or fabric; or pouring words onto paper, the involvement can take you out of yourself in a therapeutic way. When you surrender to the medium and the creative idea, you lose your ego self."

At the age of ninety-three, Pablo Casals reported that for eighty years he had always started the day by going to the piano and playing two Bach pieces. "It is a sort of benediction on the house," he declared. "But that is not its only meaning for me. It is rediscovery of the world of which I have the joy of being a part. It fills me with awareness of the wonder of life, with a feeling of the incredible marvel of being a human being. The music is never the same for me, never. Each day is something new, fantastic and unbelievable."

For example, if you have "graduated" from a recovery group, you might consider establishing a more personalized support group of your own, one that emphasizes growth and life enhancement—such as a professional group or a child-care cooperative—rather than shared dysfunction. In your new group, you can practice some of the skills you learned in twelve-step: self-disclosure, listening without judging, "being there" for others without having to fix things for them.

Remember, though, that happiness cannot be pursued actively as though it were a goal. Happiness is what happens to you while you're out there just being. If you focus too narrowly on goals, you may miss the happiness that's out there on the periphery, waiting to zoom in and zap you. Joy happens spontaneously, when you're *being* rather than reflecting on being. You never know when it will find you, or what form it will take. One thing is certain, though: You can't control it.

ENCOUNTER WITH THE WORLD

Self-expression is an essential part of the healing process, but after a point, it can look suspiciously like narcissism. Excessive focus on the inner world may result in your withdrawal from the outer world—your context, from which you are inseparable. We all need more than good relationships with ourselves; we need healthy, mutually enriching encounters with our surroundings. Victims take a narrow, restricted view; people who have developed beyond victimhood enjoy the complexity of relationship—relationship with people, with art, with the environment. Thomas Moore says, "The emptiness that many people complain dominates their lives comes in part from a failure to let the world in, to perceive it and engage it fully."

True encounter outside the therapeutic setting is much like true encounter *within* it. It is an intentional act of connection that always involves a *knowing* rather than a *knowing about* the other. As Rollo May puts it, "Encounter . . . seems to me to have a resonant character of two musical instruments. If you pluck a violin string, the corresponding strings in another violin in the room will resonate with corresponding movement of their own." Encounter is emphatically *not* the confrontation of two separate beings, batting an issue between them like a ball, with the relationship appearing to consist mostly of identifying whose court the ball is in.

Encounter is transcendent, the heart of healing. It means not only being present *with* (accompanying, witnessing) but being present *to* (engaging, attending). It means being able to look at a person or a work of art directly, with open eyes and heart, without judgment, and allowing the essence of that person or work of art to merge with you.

Of course, there is no way you can just make this happen; this is the fundamental paradox of transcendental experience. It is experience not by doing, but by not-doing, and to say "How can I achieve this?" is to assume the necessity of doing. Encounter as oneness is something you allow, not something you precipitate. I recently attended a lecture on Zen. One of the men in the audience told the speaker that he was hoping meditation would answer some of his troubling questions. It is the hoping itself, I later told him, that blocks his experience in meditation. Hoping, as a form of seeking and desiring, contaminates the process. It is only when we release our grasp that enlightenment comes.

In short, encounter is only possible by uncontaminated openness to another. We cannot make encounter and there is no "how to" to make it.

To truly encounter another human being, or the environment, is to be in tune with that person or environment. When we connect in this way, we do not victimize.

INDEPENDENCE VS. INTERDEPENDENCE

Without resonance, attunement, and authentic encounter, relationships can fall into a pattern of unhealthy conflict or dependence, both of which can make you feel like a powerless victim. Many people who want to escape the victim trap seek *independence*. This feels right; "I can do this myself" has been the mantra for our culture. Yet somehow, in our pursuit of autonomy and individualism, we leave ourselves feeling rather lonely and sad. A single voice, we learn, cannot express a chord. We feel disconnected from others, bereft of community. Ironically, we have victimized ourselves by our insistence on independence.

In days past, people used to assist one another through births, deaths, and a variety of life passages in between. They helped one another build houses, take in the crops, and tend to illnesses. But gradually we have delegated more and more responsibilities for helping one another to institutions and agencies, building up a costly bureaucracy in the process. We're busy, we have other things to do, we're not the experts after all. We have hospitals, schools, city councils, police, therapists, and lawyers to handle these things for us. Rather than providing a sympathetic ear, we urge our friends to "get into therapy" or "join a support group." When the institutions, agencies, and therapeutic cultures fail us— don't do the job we "hired" them to do—we become angry. We feel like victims because we have given away our power.

If neither dependence nor independence satisfies us, what is the answer? In a word, *interdependence*. This is not to be confused with codependence, that overused term that fundamentally means a mutual reliance on each other's failings. Interdependence implies an active acceptance of our connectedness with one another, a view of ourselves and others as inseparable, dynamically interacting parts of a larger whole.

Many recovery advocates claim that if you don't probe your unhappy childhood, you're "in denial." What most Americans are in denial about is our connection with others. We are all interdependent whether we like it or not; even such diverse factions as Israel and the PLO have come to recognize that. What hurts one part hurts the whole system, and the other parts suffer. Likewise, what's good for the individual is good for the group or community, and vice versa. Obsession about our own needs keeps us from comprehending the needs of others—and when others don't get their needs met, in the long run we won't either.

Recognizing and embracing interdependence is not always easy. It clashes—or appears to clash—with our ideas about individual responsibility. "Let those others take care of themselves—I'll take care of *my*self" has to give way to "Helping them is part of helping myself." Taking care of the "others" means caring about them. It means acting on the assumption that, as Bill Clinton put it, "there is no us and them; there is only us." This assumption did not originate with Clinton; it served as a foundation for primitive cultures and has, in modern days, been endorsed by systems theorists and even by quantum physicists. If entities have no meaning in isolation, but only in dynamic relationship with one another, interdependence cannot be denied.

THE DEVICTIMIZING QUALITY OF LOVE

If interdependence, or oneness, cannot be denied, neither can the need for love. Unity is the essence of love; love is the experience of oneness. When spiritual seekers achieve the full realization of oneness, they report they feel engulfed by an overwhelming sense of love. Couples are most in love when they feel that they are one—that the boundaries between them have dissolved.

Armed with the power of science, which has endorsed the basic oneness of the universe, I feel secure in recommending love for our social and mental health problems. I believe that the FDA should put love on its list of "fast-track" drugs because people are dropping like flies. We need love now, and in high doses. Special people (Buddha, Gandhi, Jesus, Mother Teresa, Lao-tzu) have applied love with impressive results, and the only known side effects have been reported cases of peace and joy.

Love is not caused by something or somebody ("Because of her I experience love"), and it is not dependent on other people. Goethe said, "What business is it of yours if I love you?" After all, he explained, it's his love and he'll do what he wishes with it. Love is not even dependent upon God, as many religions would have us believe. Believing that you need Jesus to come into your heart creates a dependency that distorts the pure and direct experience of love. It is not that God is love, but that love is love. It is a result of opening yourself, living as a *yes* to all of life. "Yes" connects, "no" isolates. "Yes" loves, "no" fears. "Yes" frees, "no" victimizes.

Compassion is the manifest expression of love. It goes beyond the "caring" that is considered to be an important element in any kind of therapy. Compassion, like encounter, involves feeling the other's feelings (com = with, passion = feeling), while caring implies separateness. As an instrument of love, compassion requires a surrender of the ego, and thus it flies in the face of a society that has defined itself as the playground of egos. Oneness, compassion, and love amount to a hard sell in a world that, in spite of its suffering at the hands of dualism, rejoices in its individuality and does not want to give it up. But as difficult as loving can sometimes seem, when we awaken to the truth that our separateness is only illusory, loving is the natural consequence— there is nothing left to do *but* love.

Oneness is also present within our individual selves. It is the greatest of all paradoxes that one is both an individual in the world *and, at the same time*, a pure consciousness. Bringing more awareness (seeing) into your life will lead you to love, the culmination of the experience of pure consciousness, or oneness. To the extent that you remain "in love," your actions will be saturated with it.

Love does not suggest that we smile at abusers in a saintly way. Love, however, changes the quality of the actions we take. It's tai chi rather than all-star wrestling, putting the dog out rather than throwing the dog out, setting limits rather than constructing barriers. Love affords us these changes because the experience of love is the experience of ultimate security.

Much has already been written about the ways to get to love and about the paths to transcendence. All these writings have one principle in common: The experience of the universal is a consequence of letting go of the world. Doing (compassion) is illuminated by not-doing (love). Compassion, as Ram Dass says, "is action arising from emptiness." Letting go of the world is necessary for reconnecting with it in a spirit of oneness.

Emptiness, nothingness, and the "great void" are, admittedly, difficult concepts to grasp because they resist definition. Emptiness is what is left over after dying to the world. It is the source, the background, of all that comes into being. The infinite void is pure subjectivity and therefore cannot be objectified by a definition.

It certainly is a challenge to give concrete examples of emptiness, a concept that turns our everyday way of thinking on its head. When I had my most profound experience of emptiness, one of the things I said was that nothing had changed except everything. I was a poor student, my wife had suddenly left to go find out who she was, my VW bug wouldn't run, and I had just moved to a new area where I had no friends or relatives. Yet the experience of emptiness that occurred suddenly in an evening of deep despair brought to me an indescribable peace. I had been "blessed" with what has been called the "Yoga of desperation." My pain was so great that I was willing to let go of the world completely—to trust and accept the pain. I believe those who run from it experience panic and anxiety rather than peace. They see the windows of reality (emptiness) fly open and are terrified.

Meditation is a "safer" way to little by little let go of one's attachments. The most "concrete-like" example I can suggest is to practice "seeing"; that is, attending to an object so as to experience the loss of the observer (self). The doing of not-doing is the looking without judging; it is just looking. Not-doing cleanses the doing from its cluttered prejudice.

The action that manifests from emptiness is an effortless unfolding. To understand how this works, you might try observing the contrast between making something happen and letting it happen. "Letting" doesn't imply passivity; it means allowing without effort, desire, control, desperation, or even purpose. The flower does not display its beauty for us; it simply displays.

DISCOVERING OUR ONENESS

Oneness implies wholeness, and wholeness implies the acceptance not only of our own shadow sides, but also of those differences in others that may make us uncomfortable. As we have seen, the victim business perpetuates the ideal of sameness and predictability: Being "normal" means being alike and following the same rules. But sameness is deadly, while diversity is enriching. Diversity may produce friction, as people argue for their different points of view and struggle through misunderstanding, but friction can be the spark that ignites the creative spirit.

Business organizations and civic groups are learning how to capitalize on the diverse perspectives of people who represent different ages, genders, cultural backgrounds, races, and levels of experience. Decisions reached through this kind of inclusivity are both sounder—because they are based on a synergy of broader experience—and easier to implement.

In fact, when people are *not* participants in change, they can easily come to feel victimized. They perceive that something is being done *to* them, and fail to grasp the difference between that and what the decision makers believe is doing something *for* them. Cutting people out of that decision-making process is the greatest single cause of social problems and the victimhood they engender.

But it's important to recognize that unity is not the same as oneness. A system or group that's closed becomes controlling and sometimes even cultlike. A cult differs from a community in that it is rigid, inflexible, suspicious, and heavily dependent on one leader or tight group of leaders. It avoids dissent, devalues outsiders, and promotes sameness—which sounds a bit like oneness, but is effectively the opposite. Oneness embraces differences and celebrates interdependence.

What keeps us from expressing our oneness and our interdependence is fear. We fear conflict, vulnerability, rejection, and the shadow sides of ourselves that we project onto others. We fear having to give up our individuality. We also fear failure: "It's too much responsibility—how can I possibly take care of all the social problems out there?"

The good news is that interdependence provides rewards at the same time it demands responsibility. Just ask the neighbors who take turns with child care, the employees who share planning and decision making without regard to hierarchy, the couple who consider each other's needs and the needs of the marriage as equal in importance to their own. Dozens of studies have shown that people who enjoy satisfying connections with others live longer and are healthier than those who don't.

REDISCOVERING LOST COMMUNITY

Even with a strong desire to experience community interdependence, we may not know exactly how to go about it. Here are a few suggestions:

- Enlist a few neighbors to assist you in organizing a block party.
- Offer to help a neighbor. For example: "I notice you travel a lot. Would you like me to save or throw away your newspapers when you're gone?"
- Organize a volunteer project and invite community members or coworkers to help.
- Work with other parents to form an after-school club for kids. The club could sponsor art shows, sporting events, and dances, and the kids might feel good about organizing their own community-service projects.
- Other ideas: rotating open-house parties, book discussion

groups, identifying a common problem or concern in the neighborhood that may bring people together.

Healthy individuals and healthy groups are interdependent. Giving doesn't necessarily mean giving up something—in fact, many people report that, in giving to others, they gain more than they contribute. For example, volunteer work increases life expectancy. Researchers at New York's Institute for the Advancement of Health concluded that doing good for others stimulates endorphins, those natural healers in the brain that have been linked to the "high" people get from running.

Despondent and despairing after the breakup of a relationship, Melinda, a writer and artist, began losing all sense of who she was. She was unable to afford therapy, so she turned to the exercises in a book called *The Artist's Way*. One exercise involved handwriting three pages (on any subject) a day; another prescribed weekly "artist dates" with herself, such as visits to museums or walks to new parts of the city, to "fill the well of images and experience." She also began to search for ways to use her creativity to benefit others. A friend's suggestion led her to Philanthropy by Design, a volunteer organization that procures furnishings and provides interior design services for hospices, senior and children's centers, homeless shelters, and other service centers. Soon she was happily picking colors and fabrics for a halfway house for people with mental disabilities, as well as using her writing skills to produce direct-mail appeals. Her voice became brighter, her step livelier. Both her encounters with herself and her volunteer work for others, she reported, completely took her out of her victim mode.

We've seen how victims cling to destructive labels and behaviors in part for the sense of identity and community they provide. Life after victimhood depends on reversing this behavior—rebuilding the community that we have lost.

Many people labor under the mistaken assumption that they have to fix themselves before they can attempt to improve the world. In fact, the victim business operates on the trickle-down theory that if each individual can be cured, the world will automatically improve.

This is no more logical than the seldom-questioned bromide that "I have to love myself before I can love anyone else." Since you are not separate from your context, it makes sense to pursue the healing of both at once. If you wait until you're totally okay before taking action in the world, you will never get started. And the world will continue to burden you with its dysfunction.

Sometimes it takes a crisis or tragedy, such as an earthquake, riot, or flood, to serve as a wake-up call. Such emergencies, during which people find themselves helping strangers and performing uncharacteristic and even heroic acts of selflessness, can't help but bring people together. Often, these people will then try to maintain the sense of community they have tasted, because active involvement with one another in a common effort leaves less time for despair at being victimized by tragedy. It bolsters their sense of security, acceptance, and self-esteem. "We can do this together" is a much more comforting idea than "I can do this myself." "Everything's up to us" is more empowering than "Everything's up to me" or "Everything's up to you."

A sense of meaning and freedom from loneliness depend on something broader and deeper than our relationships with ourselves and with a significant other. The self-perpetuating victim trap is a symptom, a rather embarrassing one, of an inadequate social/political system, and it is up to us, together, to break the cycle by reaching beyond the "I" to the "we."

FROM "US VS. THEM" TO "US WITH THEM"

Crime and other social crises are inviting us to become actively involved with one another, to act out love through compassion. Indeed, it *is* difficult to love that demanding, perplexing, abusive other—that victimizer or even one still mired in his or her own victim trap. But as the cartoon character Pogo said, "I have met the enemy and he is us." Taking responsibility for society is inseparable from taking responsibility for our own lives.

Blaming others keeps the focus on the past; moving on requires taking the next step: integrating the self with the wider community. All suffering is a function of polarization. And protest distracts our attention from the fundamentals of life—the deep meanings, ultimate issues, and simple truths that give substance to issues of the soul.

Blaming leads to punishing, which is the easy way out, and hardly ever the best way. When a twelve-year-old California girl named Polly Klaas was abducted and murdered by a repeat offender, her father went to Washington and demanded that the Administration push for stronger laws to keep habitual criminals in jail. The father's side of the family was so intent on punishment that they supported a state "Three Strikes and You're Out" initiative that would permanently incarcerate all felons, nonviolent as well as violent, who have been convicted three times. Later, they realized the extreme nature of this position and modified it, preferring a three-strikes measure applying to violent crimes only. Unfortunately, by this time it was too late; the Draconian measure was already on the books.

Meanwhile, Polly's mother pursued a different approach, determining to work for abused children so that they don't grow up to be abusers themselves. She had learned that the murderer, Richard Allen Davis, had exhibited the classic symptoms and background of a disturbed child, and no one had intervened. How much more sensible it is to help prevent violence from erupting in the first place than to focus entirely on punishing people after the fact.

"Identifying with criminals" is not as difficult as it sounds when you remember interdependence, oneness, and love. It has become painfully obvious that isolating ourselves from people whose behavior we abhor only creates more such behavior; those who are continually left out become antagonists. Now would be a good time to begin practicing inclusion and attunement.

Unfortunately, relatively little energy, in the victim system or in public policy, is put into preventive programs. Community support for families and children usually comes after some kind of abuse has already happened, or after a child has issued a cry for help in the form of acting out or attempted suicide. The importance of the parental role can't be overstated. Whatever form the family takes, it is the crucible within which values are forged. It is the voice of the parent that resonates within the hearts and minds of the offspring, right into the next generation.

Pablo Casals wrote, "We should say to each of [our children]: Do you know what you are? You are a marvel. You are unique. . . .

And when you grow up, can you then harm another who is, like you, a marvel? You must cherish one another. You must work—we all must work—to make this world worthy of its children."

But parents today have a hard time doing all the parenting themselves—let alone the inspiring—not least of all because in most families, both the mother and father work outside the home. Moreover, the schools are overcrowded and underfunded. And society in general does not encourage a nurturing early environment. "Who," Philip Cushman asks, "is to provide this environment? If adults are self-serving, highly ambitious, heavily bounded individuals, why would they choose to undergo the self-sacrifice and suffering necessary to be nurturing parents?"

The answer, it seems to me, is that we are all responsible. If we want a healthy environment for ourselves, it behooves us to see that not only our own children, but other people's children, have one. Otherwise, more and more victims and victimizers will be spawned. We are all in this together.

TAKING STEPS, MAKING CHOICES

Although therapeutic cultures may be cozy, they produce only a false, substitute community. Reaching for true community may require effort, in our rushed and polarized society, but it only needs to be done a little at a time. It can begin with an action as simple as phoning a couple of friends or acquaintances to plan a community-building potluck dinner. Or it can begin with a small commitment to a volunteer effort that builds homes for the homeless. I like the way *San Francisco Chronicle* columnist Jon Carroll put it:

"If you consider where love is absent, you will know what to do."

You can determine how much time and effort you put into developing community; it need not involve much more time than the time you are now putting into attending a recovery group twice a week. Each small step will vibrate the other violin strings and the web of interdependence.

As Carolyn Shaffer and Kristin Anundsen declare in *Creating Community Anywhere*, "You don't need to feel powerless in the face of the many social and planetary threats, or retreat into private community as an escape from the dangers of the wider world. Listening and speaking openly across the barriers to your friend, mate, neighbor, or co-worker are excellent ways to model—and, we believe, to effect—the changes you yearn for in the wider world."

Posters, bumper stickers, and signs on office walls in various parts of the country now sport the suggestion "Practice random kindness and senseless acts of beauty," a phrase conjured up by a California writer named Anne Herbert. Now, *there's* a simple way to build community a little at a time. Do something nice, unexpectedly, for no reason, as often as the phrase occurs to you.

If you seek a deeper sort of ongoing community, don't be afraid of the potholes along the road. Community is an open, living system, continuously affecting, and at the same time being affected by, all its members and the surrounding environment. Like other living systems (human beings, for example), it moves through stages of development. M. Scott Peck, in *The Different Drum*, posits four such developmental stages: (1) pseudocommunity, in which people act nice to one another, withhold some truths about themselves, and pretend to agree; (2) chaos, in which seemingly irreconcilable differences erupt; (3) emptiness, in which people give up struggling to control and fix; and finally, (4) true community, an authentic synergy within which individual voices are heard and listened to. Again, Emptiness—that surrendering of ego to universal consciousness, from which love emerges—is described as an essential phase.

When you become actively involved in your present context, letting go of the past and opening yourself to consciousness, love, and community, eventually you will find no room for victimism. There is too much to do. As you stand on the threshold of out-growing psychotherapy or recovery, ponder these questions:

- How do I express compassion?
- What does "reaching out to others" mean to me? Am I able to reach out even to people who are different from me? What if they belong to classes (racial, gender, family, etc.) that I feel have traditionally victimized me? Can I break the cycle by refusing to victimize them? What common ground is possible? What value can differences serve in my life?
- What can I do to assist already-organized efforts that are designed to bring various groups together?
- What can I do to create a space as safe as a recovery group or a therapist's office to hear others and be heard?
- What do I have to offer? (I am more than my labels.)
- Who needs me?
- If my family of origin has let me down, what can I do to create a "virtual family" that will provide me with nurturing and support?

- What random acts of kindness can I perform?
- What politics can replace the politics of victimhood?

Outgrowing therapy and recovery is possible only as a function of recognizing and living our freedom. The next chapter dusts off the concept of freedom and demonstrates how it powers our lives and makes meaning possible.

10

Living Your Freedom

Freedom
Man does not want freedom,
He only talks of it,
Satisfied to choose his slavery
And to pay it homage.

Freedom asks too much:
Silence and strength,
The death of empty alliances,
An end to ego baths.

Freedom confronts loneliness
And lives with it.
Makes more of larks than lust,
Builds no monuments to itself.

Freedom, content to live without goals,
Satisfied that living is enough,

Scoffs at titles, laughs at greed,
Too free to propose reforms.
Man does not want freedom,
He fears its demands,
And only needs to talk of it—
The Free Man has no such need.

But man can live without freedom,
Content to laugh at slavery
And to know today
That yesterday's pain is gone.

James Kavanaugh

Any feeling of victimization results from a perceived loss of freedom. Whether we've been mugged, verbally or physically abused, passed over for a job promotion, or abandoned by a lover, we feel that someone has taken something from us against our will. Gone is our freedom to keep our money, our self-esteem, our job opportunity, our lover. Potential choices have been snatched from us. We are at someone else's mercy; life has happened to us.

Having freedom taken from us creates a deeper wound than the stolen wallet or lost job itself. Freedom is what defines our very existence; if I don't have freedom, I am nothing, because freedom—the *way* I choose—is what distinguishes me. All other experience of myself, my personality, my meaning, my behavior follow from the fact that I am free. You mess with my freedom, you're messing with me.

We speak of living in a "free" society, and yet we have difficulty understanding freedom. Often we define it in terms of how much we get of what we want, or how much we manage to avoid getting what we don't want. We speak of it in terms of freedom *from* this or that constraint. But failure to appreciate and experience the deeper meaning of freedom leads us straight into the "powerless victim" trap.

When we are confused about freedom, we try to have *control*; when we are clear about freedom, we have a feeling of being *in charge*. Celebrating this power is, ultimately, what defines us as nobody's victim.

THE TWO FREEDOMS

Much emotional pain is caused, and prolonged, by the failure to recognize and integrate *two* types of freedom: objective freedom and subjective freedom. Objective freedom says, "I have many options available to me—possibly more than I realized at first." Subjective freedom says, "I have absolute power to choose among the options available, and to assign meaning to the world." Both kinds of freedom are necessary for emotional well-being.

When we exercise objective freedom, we are taking responsibility for our human, worldly needs. We do what we can to discover or create options that contribute to our health, comfort, happiness, and success. Americans know all about this kind of freedom: the freedom to achieve what we want. Our competitive, consumer-oriented society touts the promise of objective freedom, and the consumers of therapy, recovery, and self-help literature are testimony to the stress-producing pursuit of endless choices. We are taught to believe that with enough hard work and ambition, we can reach the top in any endeavor. Anything is possible.

And yet because, in actuality, objective choices are inherently limited, the consequence is often emotional pain, primarily anxiety and depression. When every choice is available to me, I experience complete objective freedom. Of course, since my choices are never truly unlimited, I always feel, to some extent, a victim. I may even feel that potential choices are being withheld or taken away.

Steven was complaining to me about needing food but not wanting to go to the store. "Dammit," he said, "I've got to go." I asked him why he thought he had to go. Puzzled by what seemed an absurd question, he replied, "Because I'm hungry."

Steven was suffering because he wanted food without going to the store, and felt victimized by what he perceived as a lack of choice. But he *did* have more options than he recognized. He could have called a grocery delivery service or ordered takeout from a local restaurant. That was his objective freedom.

Subjective freedom is a more difficult concept to comprehend than objective freedom. While objective freedom has to do with the number of choices I have, subjective freedom refers to my infinite capacity for choosing between or among those choices. Only I can choose, and it is the act of choosing that defines my subjective freedom. Objective freedom is limited, but subjective freedom is limitless and absolute.

"I feel really trapped," my friend Jill told me. "I have to work but I don't want to put my daughter in day care."

"Why are you putting her in day care if you don't want to?" I asked.

"I have to because there's no one else to care for her, and I have to go to my job. It's just that simple."

I agreed that it was, indeed, simple, but I didn't agree that she was trapped. "You want an income to provide for the two of you," I said, "*and* day care is the only caregiving option. Even though you don't have the choices available that you prefer, you are nonetheless exercising choice. The way I see it, it's legitimate to dislike the choices, but it's not legitimate to declare that you're trapped."

Any time you use the words *have to, should,* or *ought to,* you are not telling the truth; you are unaware of the power and anti-victimizing nature of subjective freedom. Feeling irritated by getting dressed and driving to the grocery, or unhappy about leaving your child in day care, is not a freedom problem. The problem is pretending you have no choice. Feeling victimized comes directly from the lie of lost freedom.

In order to live your freedom, you must first accept reality. "These are the choices, and given those choices, which do I choose?" Whether the option you select is pleasant or painful does not alter the fact that, given reality, this is your preference. To live your freedom, it is helpful to stop and ask yourself, "Why am I doing this?" and then notice whether, given the options, you are choosing what you really want, or whether you want to choose something else.

"I'm really upset," my patient Fred told me. "I've been offered a job in Columbus with a hefty raise, but how can I leave the Bay Area? I love it here! Still, I don't know if there's any future for me here. It's an impossible situation." I agreed that it was difficult but certainly not impossible.

"What do you mean? Of course it's impossible—I lose something important either way." I had to point out to him that he also *gained* something either way: a higher income, coupled with a richer professional future, or an opportunity to continue living in a place he loved. In any event, loss does not translate into impossibility. Fred felt victimized because he felt unfree, yet all he lacked was the freedom to expand the range of his specific choices (objective freedom), not the freedom to choose at all (subjective freedom).

Subjective freedom is Sisyphus laughing as, condemned forever, he rolls the rock up the hill. It's Felicia deciding to stay in a job she hates because the security is more important to her than job satisfaction, or Roger leaving an abusive relationship that was more painful than the pain of loneliness. Sometimes the exercise of freedom involves naming your poison—all choices may lead to outcomes that are in some way painful. But the real pain is that of feeling powerless—denying your freedom.

FIGURE 10-1. THE SOURCE AND CONSEQUENCES OF FREEDOM

SOURCE	TYPES OF FREEDOM	ACTION	CONSEQUENCES
Pure (universal) consciousness	Subjective	Creates meaning	Inherently responsible (existential guilt)
Empirical mind	Objective	Expands number of choices	Choosing to feel responsible or not responsible (neurotic guilt or victimhood)

When Sal goes to his in-laws' because he decides it's more appealing than the negative response he'd get from his wife if he didn't go, he is free with or without a smile. When Ann says, "Mary made me call her back" or "I had to give Tim a lift to the airport," she is victimizing herself. Being aware of her subjective freedom may still result in Ann's calling Mary or driving Tim to the airport. The only thing that has changed is that Ann knows she had a choice, and she doesn't feel the anguish of lost freedom. Accepting the freedom that comes along with reality eliminates the sense that we are being punished.

Most people focus entirely on restrictions to objective freedom, and that produces some rather odd responses. Body piercing, for example, is a misguided attempt to be free—to resist feeling controlled by others—but this is merely rebellion, another form of enslavement. It places control "out there." Real freedom is, "I'm *not* going to pierce my tongue, but because *I* don't want to, not because *you* don't want me to." To be nobody's victim is to live with the moment-to-moment awareness that you and you alone have absolute and total freedom to assign meaning and value to the events in your life.

In a society that confuses objective and subjective freedom, we perceive any restrictions of choice, including an act of commitment, as a threat to our freedom. When we do something we don't like, we deceive ourselves by thinking that we have lost our freedom. By understanding subjective freedom, we can freely impose restrictions on our objective freedom as a celebration of human choice.

Recall your last decision to act, or not act, in response to a situation. What was the basis for your choice? Did you fear the consequences of your actions? Did you refrain from acting out of a sense of guilt? Did you conclude that, because of guilt, for example, you were not free to act? Remind yourself of the truth. You did make a choice—perhaps not the ideal choice, and perhaps a choice between less-than-desirable alternatives, but a choice nevertheless. If you can say to yourself, "I could have told her off but I chose not to," you were living your freedom.

Once you accept the reality that objective freedom is limited— that is, you do not have an unlimited number of options—then the choosing between or among the actual options becomes an endless exercise of subjective freedom. From the moment you begin living this truth, you are forever doomed and blessed with the power to direct your own life.

Responsibility: The Dark Side of Freedom

Why did Heidegger talk about "terrible" freedom and Sartre say that we are "condemned to freedom"? Because freedom is scary. With the absolute power of freedom come some potentially terrifying truths:

1. We are alone in the world; we stand alone as the creator of meaning in our lives.
2. We must make choices without knowing the consequences.
3. Whatever the consequences of our choices, we are totally responsible.

To be courageous is to live life in the first person, to rejoice in true (objective and subjective) freedom. However, the lack of courage is not just a postmodern weakness of character, as many critics suggest, but is fundamental to the human condition. We are all naturally afraid of choosing in the face of the unknown. Limitations give us the security of boundaries. They relieve us of the burden of decision and the possibilities of choosing badly.

Although we usually talk about lack of freedom in terms of lack of choice, our freedom is challenged at times by an overwhelming number of choices. If Fred had had five job offers in the Bay Area for the same amount of money, he would have been just as crazed as he was when he thought he might have to move to Columbus. If no single best choice stood out among all the good choices, he would still be required to exercise his freedom without a guarantee that it was unquestionably the best possible choice. (That's the tricky part of this freedom business: We also have the freedom to make lousy choices.) Sometimes we oversimplify the concept of freedom because we can't deal with the infinity of choices. We suppress our awareness of absolute choice because it's overwhelming and we're not sure we're up to handling it. Responsibility is the dark side of freedom.

Like freedom, responsibility is often misunderstood. We hear public officials say, "I accept responsibility for that," as though this were a magnanimous gesture or an act of moral or ethical virtue. While in a theater line I overheard a woman saying to her friend, "Wilson just has to take full responsibility for his own feelings," which I took to mean that Wilson was trying to say that someone had *made* him feel a certain way.

But responsibility isn't something you can *take*. It is a fact, not an attitude. Since I am free—that is, I am the creator of my choices and actions—how could I *not* be fully responsible? To be free is to be unavoidably responsible. As Sartre said, "Absolute responsibility is not resignation; it is simply the logical requirement of the consequence of our freedom. What happens to me happens through me, and I can neither affect myself with it nor revolt against it nor resign myself to it. Moreover, everything which happens to me is *mine*."

In addition to denying the interdependence of all people, living your life as a victim is to practice another form of denial: the denial of your freedom. We remain in victimhood when we hide out from freedom—or, as author Erich Fromm put it, "escape from freedom." We often talk a lot about freedom, or rather our lack of it, but we do little about it, because acknowledging and honoring the existence of freedom means acknowledging the truth of responsibility.

Existential theologian Paul Tillich says that "courage is the power of life to affirm itself . . . while the negation of life because of its negativity is an expression of cowardice." Courage, then, is the virtuous act of self-affirmation. Sartre goes further still: "Those who hide their complete freedom from themselves out of a spirit of seriousness by means of deterministic excuses, I shall call cowards."

To the extent that we cling to our victimhood we are cowardly. We lack the courage to own our lives, abuses and all. We equate acknowledging responsibility with taking on blame, and since someone must be blamed when pain is caused, we would rather it be someone other than ourselves. We mistakenly think *accepting responsibility* and *accepting the fact of responsibility* are the same.

Still, referring to those of us who may feel victimized as "cowards" is an overly harsh charge in a society that seduces us into believing that the only freedom we can have is objective freedom. If the cultural assumption is that control over our lives can only come from the creation of more choices, then the feeling of victimization is not a surprising consequence.

Living your subjective freedom, with its absolute responsibility, means not feeling like a victim. It means realizing that it is not what happens to you that counts along the victimhood/empowerment spectrum, but the degree to which you exercise your freedom in response to what happens.

The up side is that freedom is undeniably worth what one has to pay in the currency of responsibility. If we understand and live our freedom, I don't think we will judge it overpriced. However, the price is never discounted; we have to pay full retail. Responsibility, like subjective freedom, is absolute.

Fred realized that no one was making him choose or not choose the Columbus job. Freedom consisted not only of a range of choices, but of the specific act of choice itself. When he was able to grasp the nature of freedom behind the issue of specific choices, he became aware of the potency of his choice-making. Rather than feeling *just* the burden of responsibility, he experienced a sense of pride in the courage he mustered in the exercise of freedom.

It is resistance and fear of freedom that cause misery and make us feel victimized. If freedom is terrible and burdensome, it is also healing and enlightening. You can never really know what's behind Door Number 3. But if you refuse to choose, or pretend there is no choice, you're off the show with no lovely parting gifts.

INTEGRATING THE FREEDOMS

Objective and subjective freedom are *both* real and important. If we denied or ignored objective freedom, we would have to detach ourselves from the real world. We would tolerate coercions, diminished opportunities, and injustices. We would demonstrate no interest in greater job opportunities and would not bother to find a food delivery service to avoid the grocery. On the other hand, if we assume that freedom is *only* a matter of having the choice or choices we want, we set ourselves up for disappointment, stress, depression, and that old victim feeling.

Since living our freedom requires constant awareness and courage, it's easier to pretend that we're not free. With its emphasis on consumerism and other quantifiable expressions of success, society encourages this pretense, focusing only on objective freedom and seducing us away from the subjective. "You aren't wealthy enough to buy a mansion, you can't have any job you want, and therefore you're not free. You need to struggle to get everything you want. If you can't, you're a victim." But the struggle is doomed to failure; the range of choices will never be great enough.

Therapy and recovery support the no-freedom pretense also— in a more subtle way—by emphasizing one form of freedom over another.

Karen told me that she had lived with her verbally abusive husband for eighteen years. He constantly criticized her, discounted her opinions, went into rages out of the blue about minor issues, and often did not speak to her for days. She lived in constant fear that she might do something to provoke one of these hurtful behaviors. She watched what she said; she tried to do everything "right" so that he would feel good. She even tolerated a lack of sexual intimacy for years, fearing to bring up the subject. When she accidentally discovered that he was cheating on her, she snapped, and even though she had very little self-esteem left, she crawled away from the relationship.

To sort things out and get her life back on track, she went to a therapist. This therapist suggested that she must have done things that provoked her husband's anger, and that, if she was ever to have a satisfying relationship, she needed to change her provoking behavior. Karen knew that this was not true—that she had made all the compromises in her care and support of her husband. So she changed therapists.

The next one told her she should simply not have "bought in" to her husband's behavior. She informed Karen that she could assign different meanings to the behavior and did not need to "take it on." "You must see his reaction to you as *his*; it belongs to him, and you can choose not to react to it," the therapist explained.

Karen tried to apply this therapist's philosophy and felt even more inadequate when she was unable to detach herself from her situation. "I guess I just can't do it. I still feel hurt and angry about the way he treated me," she lamented.

Karen's first therapist represented the view of objective freedom: "Increase your behavioral options." Her second therapist was selling the idea of subjective freedom: "If you 'reframe' what happened to you, your pain will heal. You have the God-like power to disempower the *abuse* by redefining what your husband's behavior means." Had Karen joined a recovery group, she would have also found herself in a situation that emphasized objective freedom: "If you follow these steps and change yourself, you'll recover, and everyone's reaction to you will change."

None of these approaches represented the full understanding of freedom. Increasing options (objective freedom) and exercising choice in the fact of limited options (subjective freedom) are both essential to mental health.

Living *only* one's subjective freedom lets abusive behavior off the hook. In effect, Karen would be saying, "Nothing you do or say bothers me; I have the power to decide to react to it or not. It doesn't belong to me." She would have to dissociate herself from her situation and from any part of it that intersected with the rest of her life. She could not have been her authentic self with friends, family, and neighbors who might have witnessed the abuse. But because Karen lives in the real world, she *did* feel damaged by her husband's behavior, and denying these feelings would not make them go away.

If she had insisted that "nothing you do or say bothers me," she would have been likely to carry that perspective to other relationships, thus keeping herself from authentic connection. Connection is risk, but disconnection is a form of victimization. It *appears* to place control within, but if Karen cannot be fully who she is, she is not in charge.

By not recognizing objective freedom, we live purely within ourselves; we are isolated and apart from the world. Living in the objective world, on the other hand, means being open to being affected by others. It means that being abused does matter, and we must decide to confront the situation or leave it.

But Karen is not *only* an abused wife. Her context is larger than that. She is a member of the real world, and at the same time a part of universal consciousness, where she can be an observer of the pain. Since the cosmic identity transcends worldly reality, it takes the sting out of emotional pain. It keeps pain from becoming suffering. To the extent that she is a body, she can be harmed. To the extent that she is Emptiness, she is beyond suffering. As a being-in-the-world, she has a right to her pain, but as a universal Self, she can be the painless observer. As a participant in subjective freedom, she can say, "Although abuse is real, I don't have to be a victim because of it. Within this very situation, I have choices. If I can't choose how I feel, I *can* choose what meaning the abuse has for me. I can witness my pain and move beyond it."

Those who live on the spiritual mountaintop are safe but do not participate in the world; those who live only in the marketplace are alive with feelings but do not participate in the eternal, which is the source of love and compassion. Ram Dass quotes a Buddhist monk who says, "He who clings to the void and neglects compassion does not reach the highest stage. But he who practices only compassion does not gain release from the toils of existence. He, however, who is strong in the practice of both, remains neither in samsara nor in nirvana."

Escape from victimization requires not only awareness, but living the reality of both objective and subjective freedom. We cannot ignore the reality of the effects of abuse, but we also cannot ignore the meaning-creating power of subjective freedom. Both are part of us, and emotional health means having full access to the entire range between subjective and objective reality.

PUTTING YOUR FREEDOM INTO ACTION

One way to feel victimized is to treat the past as if it were the present. Freedom is always on the move; it is a wiggly given, a whimsy you can count on. Freedom is change, and at the same time is unchanging. It is like a river, not a series of puddles, and as Heraclitus said, "You can't step into the same river twice."

Everything that is not the moment is memory, and as memory it loses reality. Memory is always at least one freeze-frame removed from the truth.

Living your freedom is moving along with reality—clarifying the difference between what was and what is. "False memory" becomes a redundancy. Memory can only be a blurred copy of the original.

While freedom flows and connects, we can dip into it and apply it to our lives. We can water this and that with it. We can decide when to opt for objective freedom and when to focus on the subjective. Usually, it's appropriate to tackle objective freedom (increasing our options) first and then move toward the subjective (choosing among the list of options we end up with). Sometimes the number of choices is adequate and the best choices are obvious. More commonly, we want more or fewer choices or to modify the ones that exist. And when no choice is good and we can't create new ones, we must accept these limits and employ subjective freedom.

Estelle was furious that her coworker Jim would not trade vacation times. After all, she had an important wedding to go to and he was just planning on hanging around town. She begged and finally threatened that he had better not need a favor from her in the future. She pleaded her case to her boss, to no avail. When she had exhausted all her attempts to change the situation, she was left angry, bitter, and feeling victimized. At that point she did not recognize that she could accept reality and then employ her subjective freedom.

When Estelle finally did exercise her power of choice, she explained to the groom and bride that she could not get time off to go to the wedding. She then booked herself and her husband on a Caribbean cruise for the vacation time she had.

As we practice awareness, we learn the rhythm of the interplay between subjective and objective freedom—creating more choices for ourselves and also, in the face of finite choices, employing our subjective freedom in the noble act of choosing while not knowing the consequences.

FREEDOM: THE MEANING MACHINE

Everywhere we hear and read about the lack of meaning in postmodern society. Observers of social and psychological turmoil point to the lack of values that would provide a stable sense of who we are. Philosophy of life has gone the way of the evanescent American dream. We feel lost, and our response has been to work the old myths harder—to reestablish "family values," to quit complaining, to put our shoulders to the task. But these efforts to revive moribund meanings only make us more anxious and depressed.

Where are the new values, then? Where are the meanings that provide us with a sense of certainty about the world and our lives? Camus offers a chilling observation: "He feels within him his longing for happiness and for reason. The absurd is born of this confrontation between the human need and the unreasonable silence of the world." The silent world throws the search for meaning back in our faces.

If meaning is not to be discovered amid this silence and unresponsiveness, then it must be created. But how can created meaning ever provide a sense of ground and certainty? If meaning is something we make up rather than something we're given, it lacks authority, and it certainly lacks comfort. And what a burden it is to have to create meaning where none presents itself. How can we be sure that the meaning we create is not just the product of some whim? We want *real* meaning.

Meaning that is *discovered* rather than created, however, comes from out there—God, social norms, political policies, etc. It produces a false sense of security because it is actually a denial or suppression of the real "given": freedom. Freedom itself is the meaning behind meaninglessness. It not only is the creator of values and meaning, it *is* the value. Living your freedom is finding meaning in the process of choosing rather than in the product of choice. Only you can assign meaning. You create your own values, including the choice to share values. Since freedom always entails responsibility, this idea may not be as freewheeling and dangerous as it first seems.

Once we understand that we have the capacity—and responsibility—for creating our own meaning, victimhood will lose its allure. Freedom is our ticket out of victimhood as well as our ticket out of the victim business. As we observe life's seemingly cruel or meager sets of choices, we can rest assured that although there is no certainty, there is still choice. The certainty of uncertainty (as disappointing as this truth may seem to be) indicates a high level of maturity—a maturity that dries our tears and breaks the victim cycle.

Using the Pause

In order to experience freedom, we must experience the moment when action is chosen out of nothing. Without the moment of "pause," as Rollo May calls it, we do not feel ourselves as the author, the chooser. "Human freedom," May says, "involves our capacity to pause between stimulus and response and, in that pause, to choose the one response toward which we wish to throw our weight. The capacity to create ourselves, based on this freedom, is inseparable from consciousness or self-awareness."

When trouble or anxiety is brewing, pausing can arm you with the awareness of options. It does not *create* options, but it does reveal them, offering the opportunity to weigh the choices that are available and make the one best suited for you.

The self-awareness pause differs from the constant state of self-reflection that the emotional health industry invites. ("Am I maximizing my potential? Am I depressed and don't know it? Am I harming my children by . . . ?") This kind of reflection leads to self-doubt. Self-doubt fuels the self-help market and sells the doubters on the absurd idea that mental health professionals are endowed with a certainty they themselves don't possess.

The moment of pause is a moment of Emptiness. You can achieve it in a number of ways—meditating in a monastery, chanting a mantra, beating a drum, fasting, praying, or simply sitting completely still in a listening mode. It is not something you learn to do; it requires not-doing. The process goes something like this:

1. Letting go of effort, struggle, analysis, and action.
2. Releasing the world and its imposed meanings.
3. Seeing and listening in the Emptiness.
4. Experiencing the feelings of reconnection and love that arise from the Emptiness.

5. Observing the full range of objective choices.

6. Feeling the limitless freedom of subjective choice.

At the end of this moment of pause, you can ask yourself,

- What do I value?
- What is the meaning of this situation—*my* meaning?
- What do I know?
- What would be the purest expression of oneness/compassion?
- What do I choose?

If you understand freedom and responsibility as they present themselves in the reflective pause, you will have integrity rather than simply *acting* with integrity.

ACHIEVING FULFILLMENT

We all have a story: a life full of both sorrow and joy. For better or worse it is *our* story, a unique set of events in the universe. To accept our story is to live in peace. Acceptance does not require an act of repentance that makes our story read better. It is saying yes to the truth, yes to the reality of "a life." The discrepancy between the life we wish we had been able to pull off and the actual life we have lived defines our suffering. It is not death that disturbs us, but remorse. It is not the successful who fear death, but the unfulfilled.

Just what does it take to define one's life as fulfilled? In America, the criteria are virtually unmeetable. We all fall short; we are never good enough. We do the best we can, though, sometimes rejoicing in the insight that existing at all is pretty miraculous.

Yet the message of our society is: "He who dies with the most toys wins." If we don't have the toys, in a panic we blame something or someone else for our toylessness. "Well, I would have had enough toys if circumstances had allowed it—if I didn't have an alcohol disease, an abusive father, a dysfunctional family, a critical mother, a boss who discriminated against me. Really, I could have achieved all that our society expects if I had just gotten the right breaks. I can't compete because I've been crippled!" The old victim wail arises from a social context.

The wail is heartfelt, though, and I cannot join in the brutal criticism of what is referred to as America's "cult of victims." In a period of time that does not contribute to essential emotional and spiritual needs, attacking people for lacking character and spunk is both shallow and unenlightening. The recovery movement holds our hand because we are hurting, and therapy pushes us to confront our own failings. Yet neither addresses the social, political, and economic contexts of our lives, nor do they walk with us into deeper recesses of the soul. We bounce back and forth between a society that does not meet our needs and a victim business that offers, at best, artificial, limited, and temporary responses to them.

The assumptions made by therapy practitioners, recovery organizations, and self-help literature render them inadequate in our search for values, meaning, love, community, and significance. They enhance our self-doubt, treat the past as present, label and pathologize, analyze, and treat causes or symptoms rather than the person as a being-in-the-world. They cannot really tell us what is wrong because they are part of the problem. Their view of humanity duplicates society's.

It seems to me that we can no longer expect either the emotional health industry or society itself to become sensitive to our unmet needs. As members of society, we must re-create society. Whatever our unmet needs are as individuals and as communities, they must be based on new myths—and here I am not using the word *myth* as a synonym for falsehood, but in its historical sense, meaning a set of cultural assumptions. We need to stop trying to breathe life into the old myths, and instead create new ones that can give us the peace and security from which to build a meaningful life. For example: "I am a universal consciousness, and at the same time, I am also an object (body) in the world. Therefore, I have absolute freedom to define my reality *and,* at the same time, to be affected by the world. I can be player and observer at once."

Could it be that the good life is not something that comes from intense mental activity or competitive struggle? If information, analysis, and "winning" were effective, we would have been cured of our emotional suffering a long time ago. It is not more data or more toys that we need but more awareness.

To help us achieve awareness, we need wise seers—men and women in tune with both the physics and mysticism of the postmodern world, who are still enough to feel the pulse of love through the roar of silence—more than we need medical-model "curing professionals." Psychology and recovery need to get out of the "how to" and "why" business and help us see the "what" of life. When we learn to see and experience rather than to analyze, to live life with our eyes open, we are free. While information and data are out there, wisdom is hard-wired within us.

As James Kavanaugh tells us in the poem at the beginning of this chapter, we too often choose slavery over freedom because "Freedom asks too much": silence (we wouldn't be able to moan on "Geraldo"), strength (we would have to acknowledge our responsibility), confronting loneliness (it's the human condition), and accepting that just living is enough (put down the toys). But our true needs can be met only through observing and experiencing—not simply believing in—simple truths like the "new myth" quoted above.

Another truth, as both physicists and mystics tell us, is the oneness behind the illusion of separateness. No longer is this concept brushed off as New Age gibberish. Letting go of our illusion unveils love as the foundation of reality. We are all victimless ripples in an ocean of waves, an ocean of love.

To know we are nobody's victim, we need to get in touch with the full range of our objective and subjective freedom. At the same time, we need to get in touch with one another.

Bibliography

....

Adam, M. *Wandering in Eden*. New York: Alfred A. Knopf, 1976.

Basch, M. F. *Understanding Psychotherapy*. New York: Basic Books, 1988.

Becker, E. *The Birth and Death of Meaning*. New York: The Free Press, 1971.

Bellah, R. ". . . Bring Along Your Compass." *The Family Therapy Networker*, November/December 1992.

Blakely, M. K. "Psyched Out." *Los Angeles Times Magazine*, October 2, 1993.

Breggin, P. R. *Toxic Psychiatry*. New York: St. Martin's Press, 1991.

Brown, E. H., and L. P. Walker. *The Informed Consumer's Pharmacy*. New York: Carroll & Graf, 1990.

Bryant, R. J. *Stop Improving Yourself and Start Living*. San Rafael, Calif: New World Library, 1991.

Burtt, E. A. *The Teaching of the Compassionate Buddha*. New York: Mentor, 1982.

Butler, K. "The Shadow Side of Therapy." *The Family Therapy Networker*, November/December 1992.

Caen, H. "Pull Cord to Stop Press." *San Francisco Chronicle*, April 15, 1994.

Camus, A. *The Myth of Sisyphus*. New York: Random House, 1955.

Capra, F. *The Turning Point*. New York: Bantam, 1982.

———. *The Tao of Physics*. New York: Bantam, 1988.

Carroll, J. "Report from the Love Summit." *San Francisco Chronicle*, February 8, 1994.

Castaneda, C. *Journey to Ixtlan*. New York: Simon and Schuster, 1972.

Chopra, D. *Quantum Healing*. New York: Bantam, 1990.

———. *Unconditional Life*. New York: Bantam, 1991.

Cormier, S. *Am I Normal?* New York: Carroll & Graf, 1993.

Cox, M. "Notes from the New Land." *Omni*, October, 1993.

Csikszentmihalyi, M. *Flow: The Psychology of Optimal Experience*. New York: Harper & Row, 1990.

Cushman, P. "Why the Self Is Empty." *American Psychologist*, May 1990.

Dass, R. *The Only Dance There Is*. New York: Anchor Books, 1974.

Dass, R., and M. Bush. *Compassion in Action*. New York: Bell Tower, 1992.

Eppsteiner, F., ed. *The Path of Compassion*. Berkeley, Calif.: Parallax Press, 1988.

Evans, P. *The Verbally Abusive Relationship*. Holbrook, Mass.: Bob Adams, 1992.

Fromm, E. *Escape from Freedom*. New York: Avon, 1965.

Gergen, K. "The Postmodern Adventure." *The Family Therapy Networker*, November/December 1992.

Goodwin, D. W. *Anxiety*. New York: Ballantine, 1986.

Hillman, J. *The Myth of Analysis*. New York: Harper Perennial, 1972.

Hillman, J., and M. Ventura. *We've Had a Hundred Years of Psychotherapy and the World's Getting Worse*. San Francisco: Harper, 1992.

Hughes, R. "Bitch, Bitch, Bitch." *Psychology Today*, September/October 1993.

Ibsen, H. *Peer Gynt*. New York: Penguin, 1982.

Joseph, J. In S. Martz, ed. *When I Am an Old Woman I Shall Wear Purple*. Watsonville, Calif.: Papier-Mache Press, 1987.

Kaminer, W. *I'm Dysfunctional, You're Dysfunctional*. New York: Vintage Books, 1992.

Kennick, W. E. *Art and Philosophy*. New York: St. Martin's Press, 1970.

Koestenbaum, P. *The Vitality of Death*. Westport, Conn.: Greenwood, 1971.

——— . *The New Image of the Person*. Westport, Conn.: Greenwood, 1978.

Krishnamurti, J. *The Awakening of Intelligence*. New York: Avon, 1973.

Lasher, M. *The Art and Practice of Compassion and Empathy*. Los Angeles: Jeremy P. Tarcher, 1992.

Lattin, D. "Therapists Turn from Psyche to Soul." *San Francisco Chronicle*, March 17, 1994.

Lawrence, D. H. *The Man Who Died*. New York: Vintage, 1953.

——— . *The Complete Poems*. New York: Penguin, 1977.

Lear, N. "Americans Are Slaves to Success While Their Spiritual Lives Wither." *The Washington Post*, May 30, 1993.

Lerner, M. "The Real Crisis Is Selfishness." *Time*, February 28, 1994.

Lukas, E. *Meaning in Suffering*. Berkeley: Institute of Logotherapy, 1986.

Maeder, T. "Wounded Healers." *Atlantic Monthly*, January 1989.

Manners, Miss. "Sympathy Means Saying You're Sorry." *San Francisco Chronicle*, January 10, 1994.

Markowitz, L. "Crossing the Line." *The Family Therapy Networker*, November/December 1992.

Marmor, J. Founder's Award lecture, 135th annual meeting of the American Psychiatric Association. *American Journal of Psychiatry*, 140:7, July 1983.

Masson, J. M. *Against Therapy*. Monroe, Maine: Common Courage Press, 1994.

May, R. *Psychology and the Human Dilemma*. New York: W. W. Norton, 1979.

———. *Freedom and Destiny*. New York: Dell, 1981.

———. *The Discovery of Being*. New York: W. W. Norton, 1983.

———. *The Courage to Create*. New York: Bantam, 1990.

———. *The Cry for Myth*. New York: W. W. Norton, 1991.

McCarthy, B. and M. *Confronting the Victim Role*. New York: Carroll & Graf, 1993.

Moore, T. *Care of the Soul*. New York: HarperCollins, 1994.

Newman, F. *The Myth of Psychology*. New York: Castillo, 1991.

Nisbet, R. A. *The Sociological Tradition*. New York: Basic, 1966.

Nozick, R. *The Examined Life*. New York: Touchstone, 1989.

Peck, M. S. *The Road Less Traveled*. New York: Simon and Schuster, 1978.

———. *The Different Drum*. New York: Simon and Schuster, 1987.

Peele, S. *The Diseasing of America*. Lexington, Mass.: Lexington Books, 1989.

Rieff, D. "Victims, All?" *Harper's* magazine, October 1991.

Rogers, R. L., and C. S. McMillin. *Under Your Own Power*. New York: G. P. Putnam, 1992.

Roiphe, K. "Fear and Feminism." *Mirabella*, August 1993.

Sagan, C. "The Search for Signals from Space." *Parade* magazine, September 19, 1993.

Sartre, J. P. *Existential and Human Emotion*. Secaucus, N.J.: Carol, 1990.

Schaef, A. W. *Beyond Therapy, Beyond Science*. New York: Harper-Collins, 1992.

Seligman, M. E. P. *What You Can Change and What You Can't*. New York: Alfred A. Knopf, 1994.

Shaffer, C. R., and K. Anundsen. *Creating Community Anywhere*. Los Angeles: Jeremy P. Tarcher, 1993.

Singer, I. *The Meaning in Life*. New York: The Free Press, 1992.

Sykes, C. J. *A Nation of Victims*. New York: St. Martin's Press, 1992.

Szasz, T. S. *The Myth of Mental Illness*. New York: Harper & Row, 1974.

Tessina, T. *The Real Thirteenth Step*. Los Angeles: Jeremy P. Tarcher, 1991.

Tillich, P. *The Courage to Be*. New York: Vail-Ballou, 1980.

Trilling, L. *Sincerity and Authenticity*. Cambridge, Mass.: Harvard University Press, 1972.

Watts, A. *The Wisdom of Insecurity*. New York: Vintage, 1951.

Weiner, B. "Bergman Harnessed His Demons to the Chariot of Art." *San Francisco Chronicle*, January 24, 1994.

Wolter, D. L. *Forgiving Our Parents*. Minneapolis: CompCare, 1989.

Yalom, I. *Existential Psychotherapy*. New York: Basic Books, 1980.

Zilbergeld, B. *The Shrinking of America*. Boston: Little, Brown, 1983.

Zweig, C., and J. Abrams. *Meeting the Shadow*. Los Angeles: Jeremy P. Tarcher, 1991.

About the Author

Christopher J. McCullough, Ph.D., is the author of *Managing Your Anxiety,* for which he received an award from the American Psychological Association for Excellence in Media. He has appeared on "Oprah," "Sally Jesse Raphael," and CNN. Dr. McCullough maintains a private counseling practice in San Francisco.